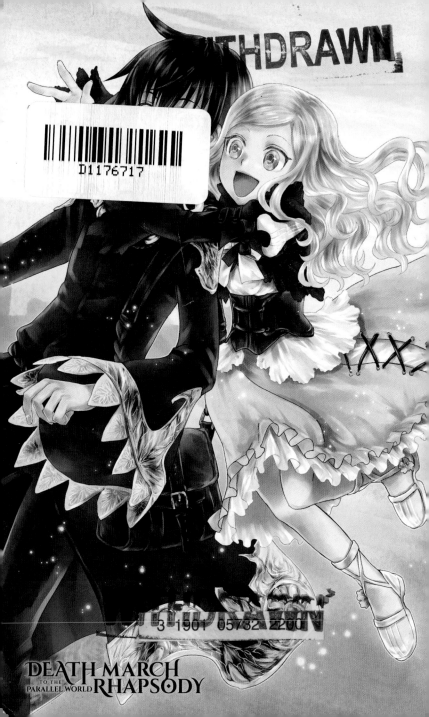

DEATH MARCH
TO THE
PARALLEL WORLD RHAPSODY

CONTENTS

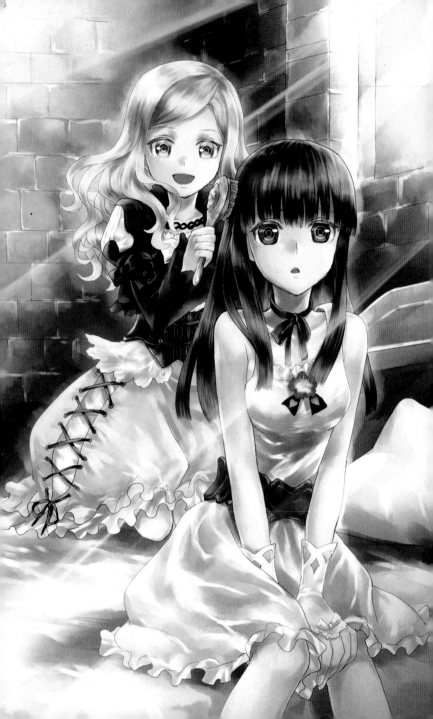

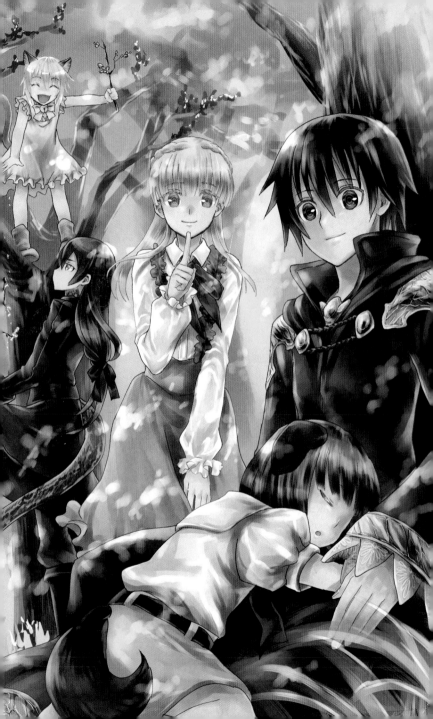

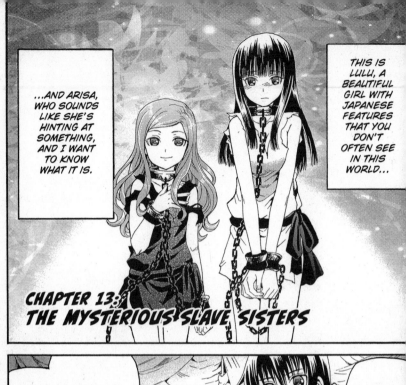

THIS IS LULU, A BEAUTIFUL GIRL WITH JAPANESE FEATURES THAT YOU DON'T OFTEN SEE IN THIS WORLD...

...AND ARISA, WHO SOUNDS LIKE SHE'S HINTING AT SOMETHING, AND I WANT TO KNOW WHAT IT IS.

CHAPTER 13: THE MYSTERIOUS SLAVE SISTERS

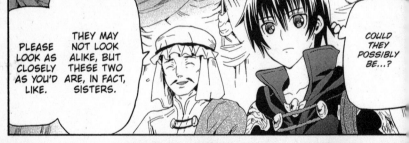

PLEASE LOOK AS CLOSELY AS YOU'D LIKE.

THEY MAY NOT LOOK ALIKE, BUT THESE TWO ARE, IN FACT, SISTERS.

COULD THEY POSSIBLY BE...?

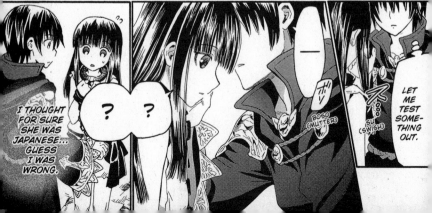

I THOUGHT FOR SURE SHE WAS JAPANESE... GUESS I WAS WRONG.

? ?

BOSO (MUTTER)

SU (SWISH)

LET ME TEST SOMETHING OUT.

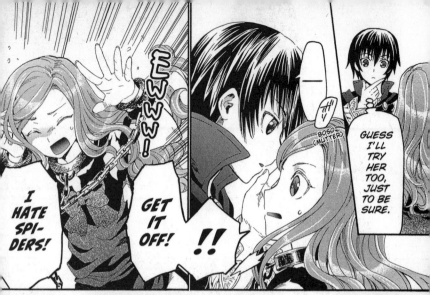

EWWWW!

I HATE SPIDERS!

GET IT OFF!

!!

BOSO (MUTTER)

GUESS I'LL TRY HER TOO, JUST TO BE SURE.

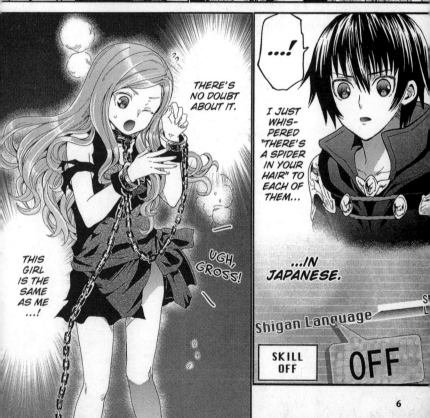

....!

I JUST WHISPERED "THERE'S A SPIDER IN YOUR HAIR" TO EACH OF THEM...

...IN JAPANESE.

THERE'S NO DOUBT ABOUT IT.

UGH, GROSS!

THIS GIRL IS THE SAME AS ME ...!

Shigan Language

SKILL OFF

OFF

6

...I WILL ALWAYS SERVE MY MASTER WITH ALL OF MY POWER.

AT ALL TIMES, DAY OR NIGHT...

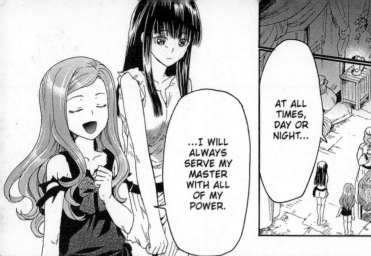

I JUST WANT TO KNOW WHAT INFORMATION ARISA HAS...

IS SHE TRYING TO IMPRESS ME?

IN THE END...

...I WOUND UP SIGNING A SLAVERY CONTRACT WITH BOTH LULU AND ARISA.

SKILL ACQUIRED: "CONTRACT"

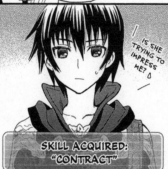

I GUESS I'LL LOOK INTO IT AGAIN SOME OTHER TIME.

DON'T LEAVE US!

HE SAID THAT FREE DEMI-HUMANS WOULD BE TREATED EVEN WORSE THAN SLAVES IN A PLACE WITH SUCH INTENSE HATRED FOR THEM LIKE THIS ONE.

I TRIED TO FREE THE BEAST-FOLK GIRLS FROM THEIR STATUS AS SLAVES, BUT NIDOREN STOPPED ME.

WELL, I'M PLANNING TO RELEASE THEM FROM SLAVERY ONCE I GET THAT INFORMATION, SO IT'S PROBABLY BEST TO KEEP THE SISTERS TOGETHER.

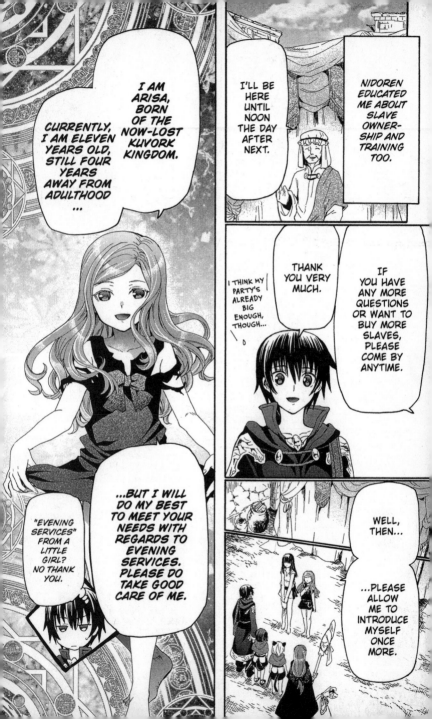

I AM ARISA, BORN OF THE NOW-LOST KUVORK KINGDOM.

CURRENTLY, I AM ELEVEN YEARS OLD, STILL FOUR YEARS AWAY FROM ADULTHOOD...

I'LL BE HERE UNTIL NOON THE DAY AFTER NEXT.

NIDOREN EDUCATED ME ABOUT SLAVE OWNER-SHIP AND TRAINING TOO.

THANK YOU VERY MUCH.

I THINK MY PARTY'S ALREADY BIG ENOUGH, THOUGH...

IF YOU HAVE ANY MORE QUESTIONS OR WANT TO BUY MORE SLAVES, PLEASE COME BY ANYTIME.

..BUT I WILL DO MY BEST TO MEET YOUR NEEDS WITH REGARDS TO EVENING SERVICES. PLEASE DO TAKE GOOD CARE OF ME.

"EVENING SERVICES" FROM A LITTLE GIRL? NO THANK YOU.

WELL, THEN...

...PLEASE ALLOW ME TO INTRODUCE MYSELF ONCE MORE.

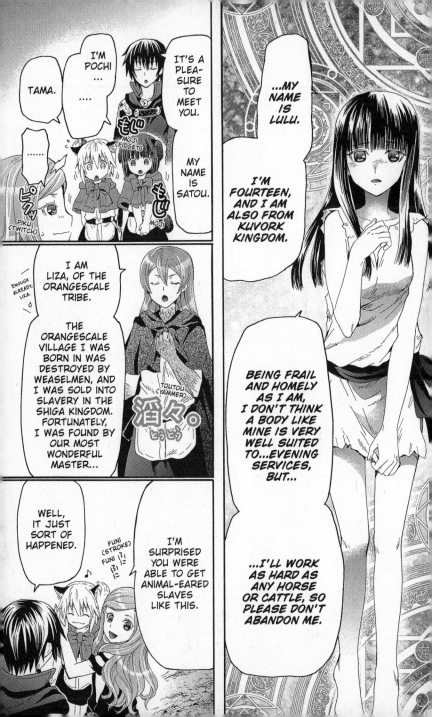

TAMA.

I'M POCHI...

.....

......

IT'S A PLEASURE TO MEET YOU.

MY NAME IS SATOU.

MOSO (FIDGET)

PIKU (TWITCH)

MOSO

I AM LIZA, OF THE ORANGESCALE TRIBE.

ENOUGH ALREADY, LIZA.

THE ORANGESCALE VILLAGE I WAS BORN IN WAS DESTROYED BY WEASELMEN, AND I WAS SOLD INTO SLAVERY IN THE SHIGA KINGDOM. FORTUNATELY, I WAS FOUND BY OUR MOST WONDERFUL MASTER...

TOUTOLI (YAMMER)

滔々。

WELL, IT JUST SORT OF HAPPENED.

FUNI (STROKE) FUNI

I'M SURPRISED YOU WERE ABLE TO GET ANIMAL-EARED SLAVES LIKE THIS.

...MY NAME IS LULU.

I'M FOURTEEN, AND I AM ALSO FROM KUVORK KINGDOM.

BEING FRAIL AND HOMELY AS I AM, I DON'T THINK A BODY LIKE MINE IS VERY WELL SUITED TO...EVENING SERVICES, BUT...

...I'LL WORK AS HARD AS ANY HORSE OR CATTLE, SO PLEASE DON'T ABANDON ME.

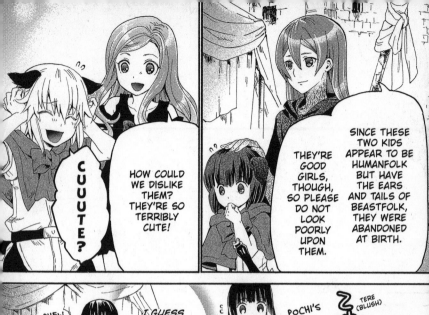

CUUUTE?

HOW COULD WE DISLIKE THEM? THEY'RE SO TERRIBLY CUTE!

THEY'RE GOOD GIRLS, THOUGH, SO PLEASE DO NOT LOOK POORLY UPON THEM.

SINCE THESE TWO KIDS APPEAR TO BE HUMANFOLK BUT HAVE THE EARS AND TAILS OF BEASTFOLK, THEY WERE ABANDONED AT BIRTH.

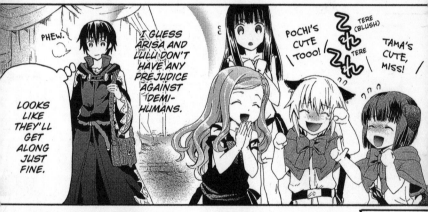

PHEW.

I GUESS ARISA AND LULU DON'T HAVE ANY PREJUDICE AGAINST DEMI-HUMANS.

LOOKS LIKE THEY'LL GET ALONG JUST FINE.

POCHI'S CUTE TOOO!

TERE TERE TERE (BLUSH)

TAMA'S CUTE, MISS!

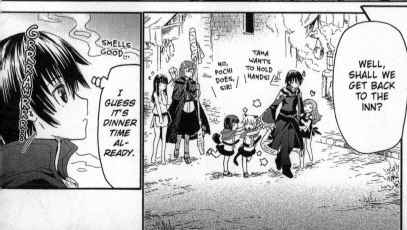

SMELLS GOOD...

I GUESS IT'S DINNER TIME AL-READY.

GRRRAWRRRR

NO, POCHI DOES, SIR!

TAMA WANTS TO HOLD HANDS!

WELL, SHALL WE GET BACK TO THE INN?

MEAT WOULD BE GOOD, SIR!

MEAT?

WHAT DO YOU WANT TO EAT?

WHY DON'T WE GET SOME DINNER HERE BEFORE WE GO BACK?

PYON (BOUNCE)

IF I MAY DARE TO MAKE A SUGGESTION, I BELIEVE CHICKEN MEAT WOULD BE TRULY DIVINE.

OH, RIGHT.

HE'S ONE OF THE MEN WE RESCUED FROM THE SLIME.

THAT MAN APPEARS TO BE CALLING YOU...

YOUNG MAS-TER!

HM?

I SMELL SOME KIND OF MEAT-BASED DISH, SO MOST IMPORTANTLY, I'M SURE THE BEASTFOLK GIRLS WILL LIKE IT!

I GUESS WE MIGHT AS WELL EAT HERE.

THE YOUNG LADIES CAN EAT TOO, OF COURSE!

YOUNG MASTER, PLEASE COME HAVE SOME FOOD IF YOU'D LIKE!

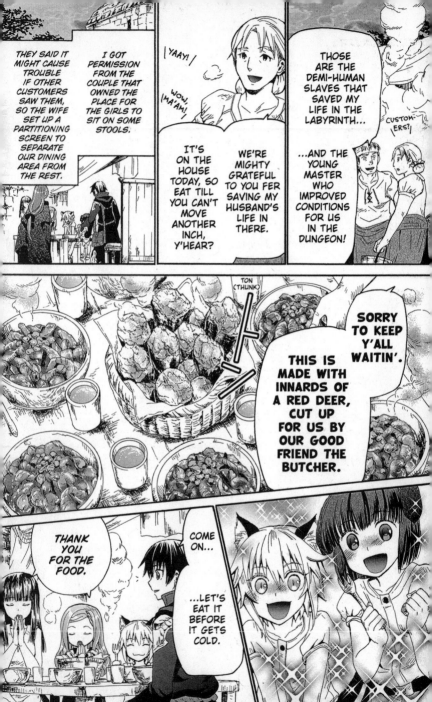

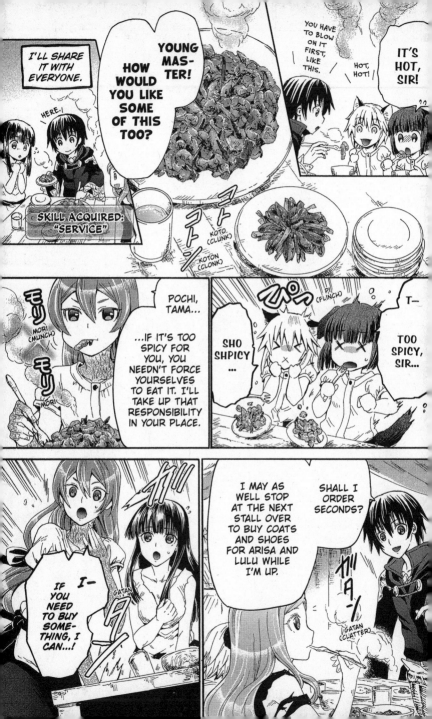

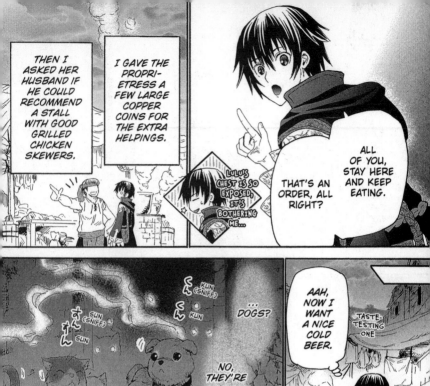

THEN I ASKED HER HUSBAND IF HE COULD RECOMMEND A STALL WITH GOOD GRILLED CHICKEN SKEWERS.

I GAVE THE PROPRIETRESS A FEW LARGE COPPER COINS FOR THE EXTRA HELPINGS.

LULU'S CHEST IS SO EXPOSED, IT'S BOTHERING ME...

THAT'S AN ORDER, ALL RIGHT?

ALL OF YOU, STAY HERE AND KEEP EATING.

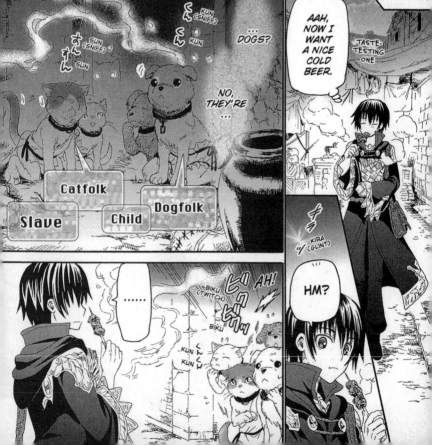

すん (SNIFF) SUN

すん (SNIFF) SUN

くん KUN (SNIFF)

くん KUN

...DOGS?

NO, THEY'RE...

AAH, NOW I WANT A NICE COLD BEER.

TASTE-TESTING ONE

Catfolk

Slave

Child

Dogfolk

キラ KIRA (GLINT)

......

AH!

ビク (TWITCH)

ビク BIKU

ビク BIKU

くん KUN

くん KUN

HM?

♪♪♪

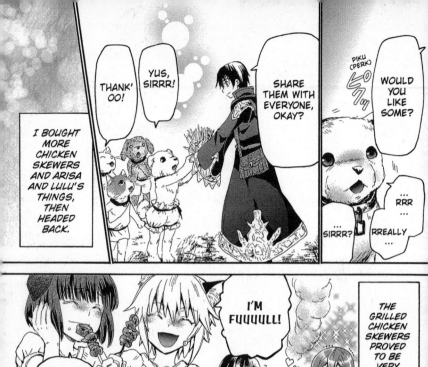

I BOUGHT MORE CHICKEN SKEWERS AND ARISA AND LULU'S THINGS, THEN HEADED BACK.

THANK' OO!

YUS, SIRRR!

SHARE THEM WITH EVERYONE, OKAY?

PIKU (PERK)

WOULD YOU LIKE SOME?

...SIRRR?

RREALLY...

...RRR...

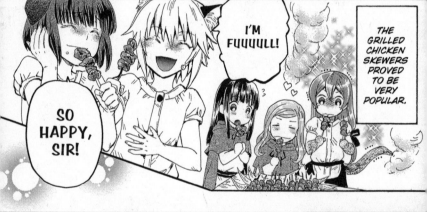

I'M FUUUULL!

THE GRILLED CHICKEN SKEWERS PROVED TO BE VERY POPULAR.

SO HAPPY, SIR!

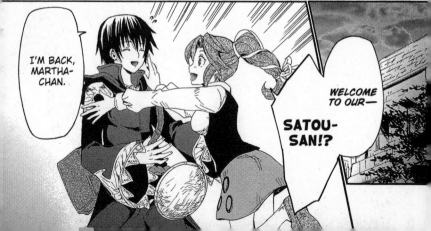

I'M BACK, MARTHA-CHAN.

WELCOME TO OUR—

SATOU-SAN!?

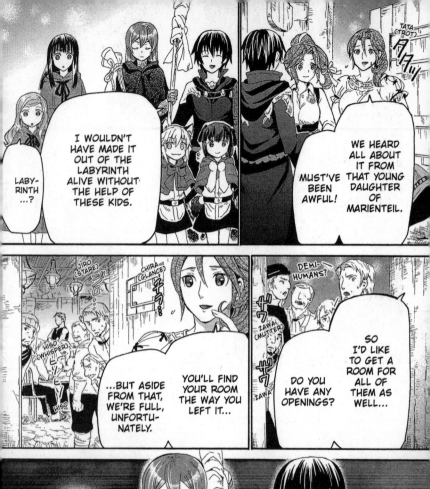

LABY-RINTH...?

I WOULDN'T HAVE MADE IT OUT OF THE LABYRINTH ALIVE WITHOUT THE HELP OF THESE KIDS.

MUST'VE BEEN AWFUL!

WE HEARD ALL ABOUT IT FROM THAT YOUNG DAUGHTER OF MARIENTEIL.

JIRO (STARE)

CHIRA (GLANCE)

HISO (WHISPER)

HISO

...BUT ASIDE FROM THAT, WE'RE FULL, UNFORTUNATELY.

YOU'LL FIND YOUR ROOM THE WAY YOU LEFT IT...

DEMI-HUMANS?

ZAWA (MUTTER)

ZAWA

DO YOU HAVE ANY OPENINGS?

SO I'D LIKE TO GET A ROOM FOR ALL OF THEM AS WELL...

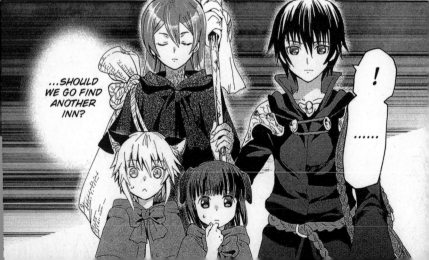

...SHOULD WE GO FIND ANOTHER INN?

!

......

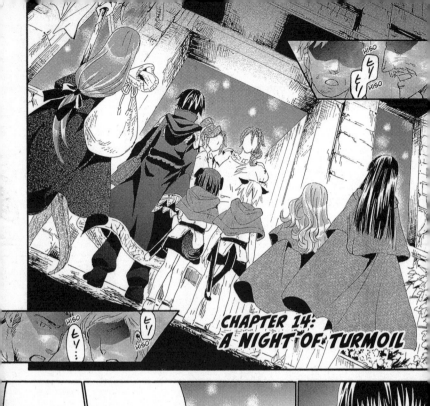

HISO
ヒソ
HISO

HISO
ヒソ
ヒソ
HISO...

CHAPTER 14: A NIGHT OF TURMOIL

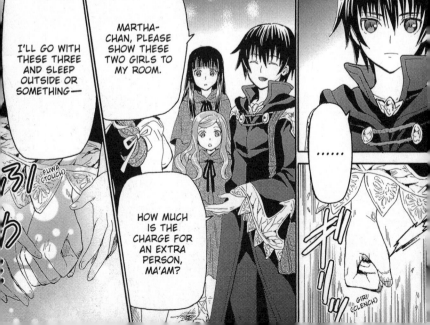

I'LL GO WITH THESE THREE AND SLEEP OUTSIDE OR SOMETHING—

MARTHA-CHAN, PLEASE SHOW THESE TWO GIRLS TO MY ROOM.

HOW MUCH IS THE CHARGE FOR AN EXTRA PERSON, MA'AM?

......

FUWA (TOUCH)

GIRI (CLENCH)

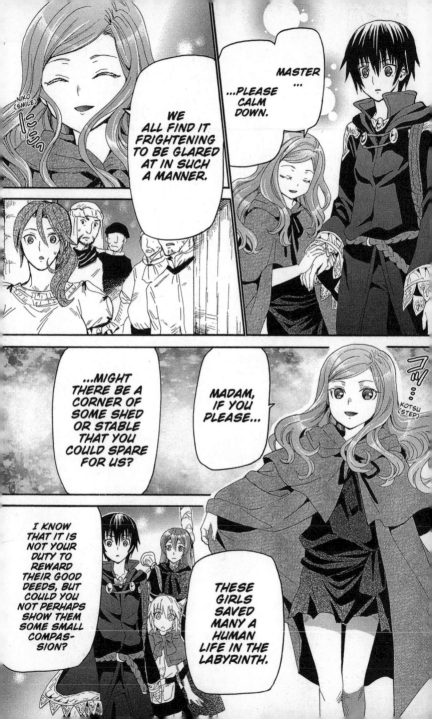

NIKO (SMILE)

MASTER...

...PLEASE CALM DOWN.

WE ALL FIND IT FRIGHTENING TO BE GLARED AT IN SUCH A MANNER.

...MIGHT THERE BE A CORNER OF SOME SHED OR STABLE THAT YOU COULD SPARE FOR US?

MADAM, IF YOU PLEASE...

KOTSU (STEP)

I KNOW THAT IT IS NOT YOUR DUTY TO REWARD THEIR GOOD DEEDS, BUT COULD YOU NOT PERHAPS SHOW THEM SOME SMALL COMPASSION?

THESE GIRLS SAVED MANY A HUMAN LIFE IN THE LABYRINTH.

THAT WAS A LETDOWN, HUH?

R-RIGHT...

ZAWA (CHATTER)

ZAWA

LET'S DRINK SOME MORE.

WE DON'T HAVE TOO MANY GUESTS WITH HORSES OR CARTS RIGHT NOW, SO THERE OUGHT TO BE SOME ROOM IN THE STABLE.

MARTHA, SHOW THEM THE WAY.

A... ALL RIGHT...

SHOULD HEAD OUT SOON.

ZAWA
ZAWA

THAT SURE BLEW OVER EASILY...

CAN YOU ORDER FOR ME?

SATOU-SAN...

...WE'LL BRING ANOTHER BED UP TO YOUR ROOM.

ZAWA
ZAWA

FLUFFYYY!

NIKO

THANK YOU.

YEAH, YOU WERE A BIG HELP.

WELL, WAS I ABLE TO BE OF SOME USE TO YOU?

...SHE LOOKS PRETTY PALE...

YAWN...

I WANTED TO ASK ARISA ABOUT WHY SHE KNOWS JAPANESE AND ALL, BUT...

OH, NO, NOT AT ALL.

SORRY I TOOK SO LONG.

BATAN (SHUT)

SHOULD WE JUST GO TO BED NOW?

IT'S NOT LIKE THERE'S ANY PARTICULAR NEED TO RUSH.

DOKI (BADUMP)

IT'S ALL RIGHT. I DON'T NEED HELP.

YOU TWO JUST GET READY FOR BED YOUR-SELVES.

.......!

HMM?

GA (THUD)

Y...

YES, SIR...

KAA (BLUSH)

Y... YES, I'M FINE!

I'M PERFECTLY FINE!

ARE YOU ALL RIGHT?

AAAH!

ドサ
DOSA
(WHUMP)

！

I THINK LULU MIGHT BE A LITTLE UNCOMFORTABLE WITH MEN.

ARE YOU SURE...?

...WE'RE READY!

...ACTUALLY, I GUESS THIS IS A PRETTY NORMAL REACTION...

...SINCE I'M STILL A STRANGER TO HER.

ニュル...
SHURU
(SLIP)

シュル
SHURU

パサ
PASA
(RUSTLE)

U-UM, BUT...

...YOUR SERVICES...

YOU CAN WEAR THE LONG SHIRTS I GAVE YOU EARLIER AS NIGHTGOWNS.

...THESE BLANKETS ARE PRETTY THIN, SO YOU'LL CATCH A COLD IF YOU DON'T WEAR ANYTHING TO BED.

LISTEN, GIRLS...

I'M GOING TO HAVE YOU TWO GO BUY YOURSELVES SOME NECESSITIES TOMORROW MORNING...

...SO PLEASE GO TO BED NOW...

I DON'T NEED ANY.

YOU DON'T NEED ANY!?

GAN
(CRASH)

OH, LULU...

IF THEY WERE ADULT WOMEN, I MIGHT HAVE COME CLOSE TO GIVING IT A THOUGHT...

...BUT I'M DEFINITELY NOT GOING TO DO ANYTHING TO A CHILD.

I WON'T BE NEEDING THAT KIND OF SERVICE IN THE FUTURE EITHER.

...LOOKS LIKE THEY'RE ASLEEP.

GOSO (RUSTLE)
ゴソゴソ
GOSO

ZZZ...

WAS THAT MY IMAGINATION...?

HMM?

HMPH!

FASA (SWISH)

ファサ...

I'M PRETTY EXHAUSTED MYSELF.

GUESS I'LL TURN IN TOO.

GUESS I'LL TURN IT OFF.

EVEN WITH MY EYES CLOSED, I CAN STILL SEE THE MENU...

MENU

N W E S

......

HEH

フィ

HEH

フィ

HMM ...?

WHAT'S THIS WEIRD FEELING?

YOU WANT HER...

SINCE WHEN AM I ATTRACTED TO LITTLE GIRLS?

...I DON'T REMEMBER SHARING A BED WITH ARISA.

WEIRD...

KUSU (GIGGLE)

KUSU

THERE'S NO WAY I WOULD EVER...

...REACT TO A LITTLE KID LIKE THIS.

SHE'S SO CUTE...

MAYBE THERE'S SOMETHING IN THE LOG THAT...

I'LL OPEN THE MENU.

PA (SHINE)

SHE'D PROBABLY USED THOSE TO CALM THE HATRED THE CROWD FELT TOWARD THE BEASTFOLK GIRLS.

CALM FIELD AND WEARINESS FIELD...

THE FIRST TIME WAS OUTSIDE THE INN.

SHE'S ALREADY USED HER MAGIC TWICE.

CHARM PERSON, TEMPTATION FIELD, AND LUSTING HEART FIELD...

...THE SECOND TIME, THE SPELLS SHE USED ON ME JUST NOW WERE...

THAT'S ALL WELL AND GOOD, BUT...

...PSYCHIC MAGIC? I DON'T KNOW WHAT YOU MEAN...

IT SAID "UNKNOWN."

I DIDN'T NOTICE BEFORE, BUT HER A.R. INFORMATION DIDN'T SAY "NONE" FOR HER SKILLS...

TITLES: Witch of the Lost Kingdom The Mad Princess
SKILLS: Unknown

CLEARLY, SHE WAS TRYING TO SEDUCE ME AND BEND ME TO HER WILL.

SKILL ACQUIRED: "INTERROGATION"

WHAT IS IT THAT YOU WANT? TELL ME THE TRUTH.

ZZZ...

PERFECT TIMING.

I'LL ACTIVATE THAT RIGHT NOW.

NOW, WHAT WERE YOU TRYING TO DO?

DON'T TRY TO TRICK ME OR PLAY DUMB. THAT'S ANOTHER ORDER.

REALLY! DON'T YOU GET IT BY NOW!?

I DON'T UNDERSTAND. EXPLAIN YOURSELF.

....
....

THE FIRST TIME WE MET, I FELL IN LOVE WITH YOU AT FIRST SIGHT!

HUH?

...I JUST WANTED TO SERVE YOU, MASTER.

32

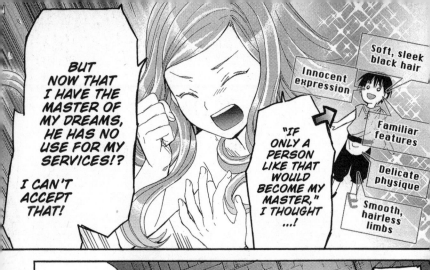

BUT NOW THAT I HAVE THE MASTER OF MY DREAMS, HE HAS NO USE FOR MY SERVICES!?

I CAN'T ACCEPT THAT!

"IF ONLY A PERSON LIKE THAT WOULD BECOME MY MASTER," I THOUGHT...!

Soft, sleek black hair

Innocent expression

Familiar features

Delicate physique

Smooth, hairless limbs

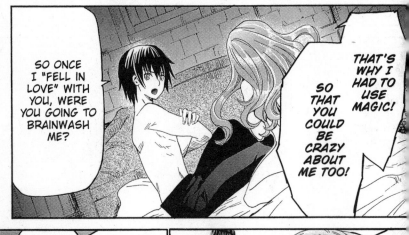

SO ONCE I "FELL IN LOVE" WITH YOU, WERE YOU GOING TO BRAINWASH ME?

SO THAT YOU COULD BE CRAZY ABOUT ME TOO!

THAT'S WHY I HAD TO USE MAGIC!

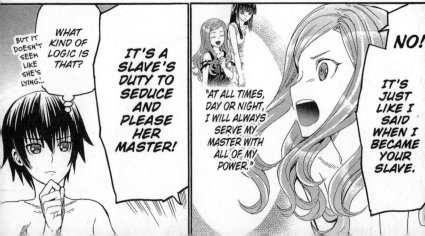

WHAT KIND OF LOGIC IS THAT?

BUT IT DOESN'T SEEM LIKE SHE'S LYING...

IT'S A SLAVE'S DUTY TO SEDUCE AND PLEASE HER MASTER!

"AT ALL TIMES, DAY OR NIGHT, I WILL ALWAYS SERVE MY MASTER WITH ALL OF MY POWER."

NO!

IT'S JUST LIKE I SAID WHEN I BECAME YOUR SLAVE.

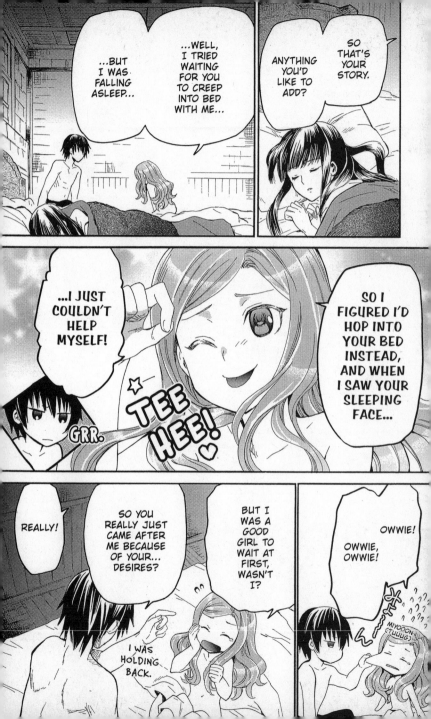

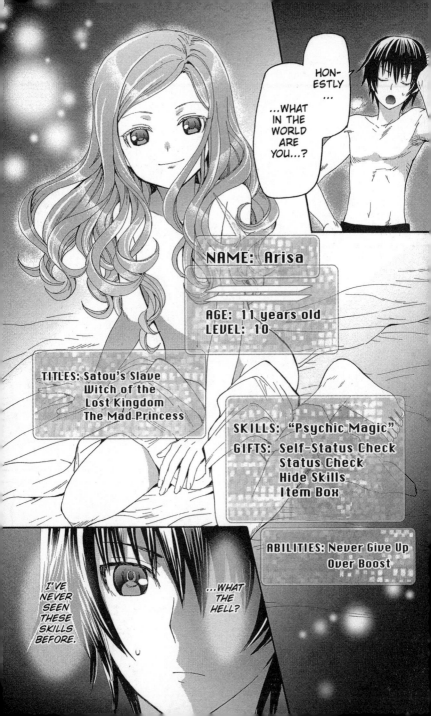

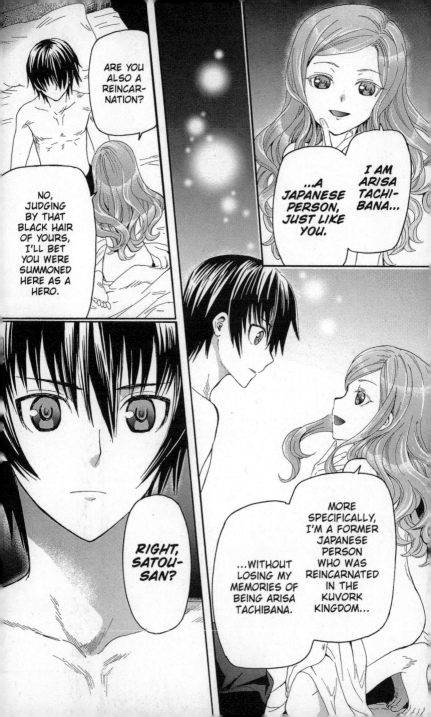

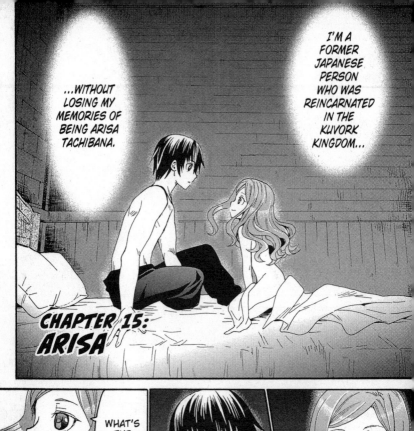

I'M A FORMER JAPANESE PERSON WHO WAS REINCARNATED IN THE KUVORK KINGDOM...

...WITHOUT LOSING MY MEMORIES OF BEING ARISA TACHIBANA.

CHAPTER 15: ARISA

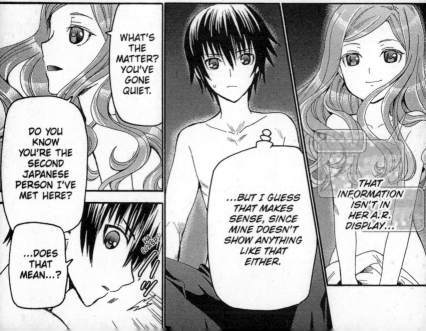

WHAT'S THE MATTER? YOU'VE GONE QUIET.

DO YOU KNOW YOU'RE THE SECOND JAPANESE PERSON I'VE MET HERE?

...DOES THAT MEAN...?

...BUT I GUESS THAT MAKES SENSE, SINCE MINE DOESN'T SHOW ANYTHING LIKE THAT EITHER.

THAT INFORMATION ISN'T IN HER A.R. DISPLAY...

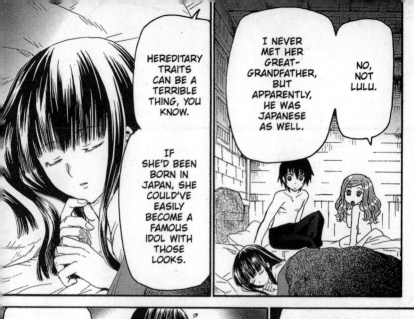

NO, NOT LULU.

I NEVER MET HER GREAT-GRANDFATHER, BUT APPARENTLY, HE WAS JAPANESE AS WELL.

HEREDITARY TRAITS CAN BE A TERRIBLE THING, YOU KNOW.

IF SHE'D BEEN BORN IN JAPAN, SHE COULD'VE EASILY BECOME A FAMOUS IDOL WITH THOSE LOOKS.

WHAT DO YOU MEAN?

SHE WAS SPEAKING POORLY OF HERSELF, BUT SHE MUST BE POPULAR IN THE SHIGA KINGDOM TOO, RIGHT?

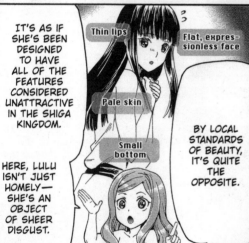

Thin lips

Flat, expressionless face

Pale skin

Small bottom

IT'S AS IF SHE'S BEEN DESIGNED TO HAVE ALL OF THE FEATURES CONSIDERED UNATTRACTIVE IN THE SHIGA KINGDOM.

HERE, LULU ISN'T JUST HOMELY— SHE'S AN OBJECT OF SHEER DISGUST.

BY LOCAL STANDARDS OF BEAUTY, IT'S QUITE THE OPPOSITE.

I'M NOT SURPRISED YOU WOULD THINK THAT.

BUT TO THE PEOPLE IN THIS WORLD, THAT GIRL ISN'T BEAUTIFUL AT ALL.

...HUH? THEN AM I...?

YOU WON'T EXACTLY BE CONSIDERED HANDSOME...

...BUT I THINK THEY JUST SEE YOU AS A NORMAL FOREIGNER.

I SEE...

AS YOU WISH, MASTER.

I'M GONNA FORGET MY REAL NAME...

STOP CALLING ME THAT, PLEASE.

SO, SATOU-SAN!

ARE YOU A TRANSMIGRA-TION OR A TRANSFERENCE?

UH...

...WHAT'S THE DIFFERENCE?

SO WHICH IS IT, MASTER?

DO TRANS-MIGRATIONS ALWAYS START AS BABIES?

YES, IN THIS WORLD, IT ONLY HAPPENS WITH BABIES.

THAT'S WHAT THE GOD TOLD ME WHEN I WAS REINCARNATED HERE.

A *TRANS-MIGRATION* IS A SOUL THAT DIED EARLY IN AN ACCIDENT OR THE LIKE IN THE REAL WORLD AND WAS REINCARNATED IN THIS ONE.

A *TRANSFERENCE* IS SOMEONE WHO WAS ABDUCTED INTO THIS WORLD AGAINST THEIR WILL BY SUMMONING MAGIC.

HEROES, FOR EXAMPLE.

HUH...? GOD...?

SHE MET A GOD?

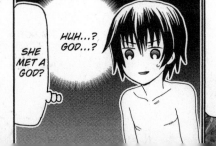
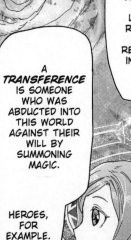
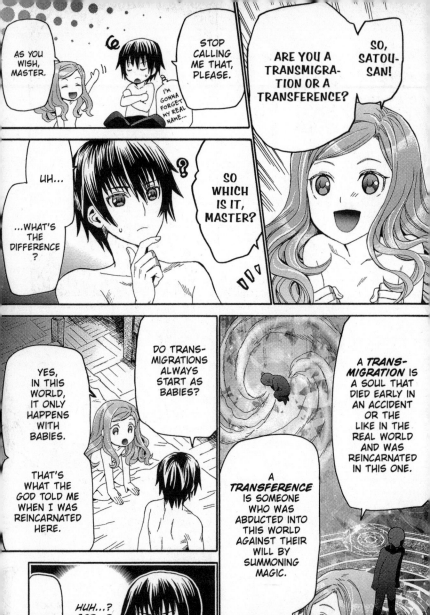

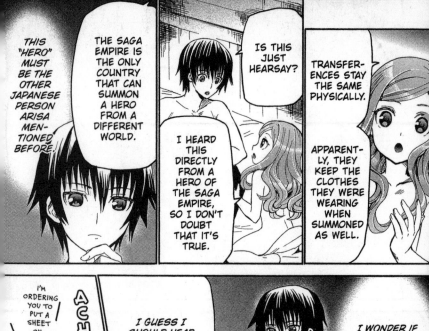

THIS "HERO" MUST BE THE OTHER JAPANESE PERSON ARISA MENTIONED BEFORE.

THE SAGA EMPIRE IS THE ONLY COUNTRY THAT CAN SUMMON A HERO FROM A DIFFERENT WORLD.

IS THIS JUST HEARSAY?

I HEARD THIS DIRECTLY FROM A HERO OF THE SAGA EMPIRE, SO I DON'T DOUBT THAT IT'S TRUE.

TRANSFERENCES STAY THE SAME PHYSICALLY.

APPARENTLY, THEY KEEP THE CLOTHES THEY WERE WEARING WHEN SUMMONED AS WELL.

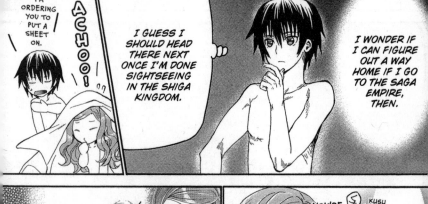

I'M ORDERING YOU TO PUT A SHEET ON.

ACHOO!

I GUESS I SHOULD HEAD THERE NEXT ONCE I'M DONE SIGHTSEEING IN THE SHIGA KINGDOM.

I WONDER IF I CAN FIGURE OUT A WAY HOME IF I GO TO THE SAGA EMPIRE, THEN.

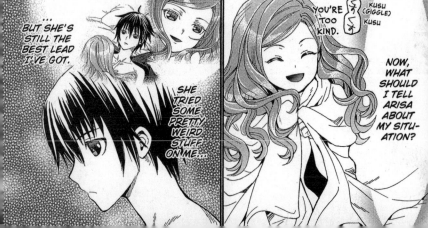

...BUT SHE'S STILL THE BEST LEAD I'VE GOT.

SHE TRIED SOME PRETTY WEIRD STUFF ON ME...

YOU'RE TOO KIND.

KUSU (GIGGLE) KUSU

NOW, WHAT SHOULD I TELL ARISA ABOUT MY SITUATION?

...AND WHEN I WOKE UP, I WAS STANDING IN A BIG WASTELAND.

I WAS TAKING A NAP AT MY WORKPLACE...

...BUT I MIGHT NOT BE EITHER OF THOSE.

I SEE...

YOU DIDN'T MEET A GOD?

NO SUCH LUCK.

THEN DID YOU START AT A HIGH LEVEL?

WITH INFINITE MAGIC?

OR TONS OF SKILLS?

NO, I STARTED AT LEVEL ONE...

...AND I ONLY HAD TEN MAGIC POINTS AND NO SKILLS.

SO YOU CAME OUT IN THE MIDDLE OF A SUMMONING CIRCLE WHEN YOU GOT HERE, THEN, RIGHT?

NOPE.

I WAS ALL BY MYSELF.

NOW SHE FEELS BAD FOR ME?

THAT SEEMS UNREASONABLY CHALLENGING.

REALLY?

...OH...

...I GUESS I DID HAVE THE LIMITED-USE METEOR SHOWER ICONS AND ALL.

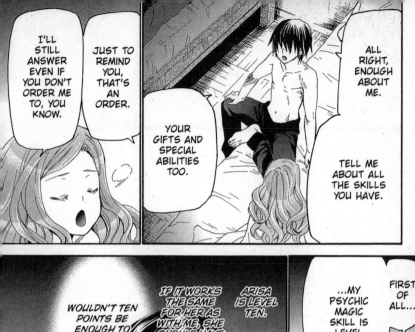

I'LL STILL ANSWER EVEN IF YOU DON'T ORDER ME TO, YOU KNOW.

JUST TO REMIND YOU, THAT'S AN ORDER.

YOUR GIFTS AND SPECIAL ABILITIES TOO.

ALL RIGHT, ENOUGH ABOUT ME.

TELL ME ABOUT ALL THE SKILLS YOU HAVE.

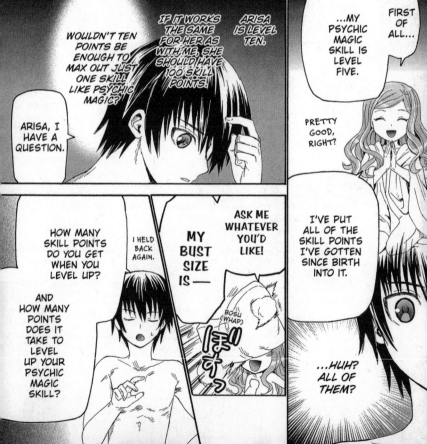

WOULDN'T TEN POINTS BE ENOUGH TO MAX OUT JUST ONE SKILL LIKE PSYCHIC MAGIC?

IF IT WORKS THE SAME FOR HER AS WITH ME, SHE SHOULD HAVE 100 SKILL POINTS!

ARISA IS LEVEL TEN.

ARISA, I HAVE A QUESTION.

...MY PSYCHIC MAGIC SKILL IS LEVEL FIVE.

FIRST OF ALL...

PRETTY GOOD, RIGHT?

HOW MANY SKILL POINTS DO YOU GET WHEN YOU LEVEL UP?

AND HOW MANY POINTS DOES IT TAKE TO LEVEL UP YOUR PSYCHIC MAGIC SKILL?

I HELD BACK AGAIN.

MY BUST SIZE IS—

ASK ME WHATEVER YOU'D LIKE!

BOSU (WHAP)

I'VE PUT ALL OF THE SKILL POINTS I'VE GOTTEN SINCE BIRTH INTO IT.

...HUH? ALL OF THEM?

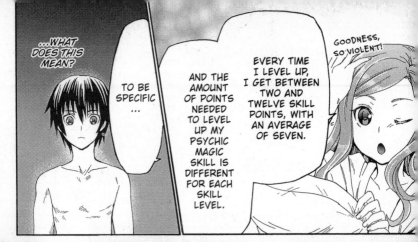

...WHAT DOES THIS MEAN?

TO BE SPECIFIC...

AND THE AMOUNT OF POINTS NEEDED TO LEVEL UP MY PSYCHIC MAGIC SKILL IS DIFFERENT FOR EACH SKILL LEVEL.

EVERY TIME I LEVEL UP, I GET BETWEEN TWO AND TWELVE SKILL POINTS, WITH AN AVERAGE OF SEVEN.

GOODNESS, SO VIOLENT!

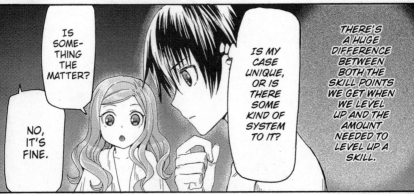

IS SOMETHING THE MATTER?

NO, IT'S FINE.

IS MY CASE UNIQUE, OR IS THERE SOME KIND OF SYSTEM TO IT?

THERE'S A HUGE DIFFERENCE BETWEEN BOTH THE SKILL POINTS WE GET WHEN WE LEVEL UP AND THE AMOUNT NEEDED TO LEVEL UP A SKILL.

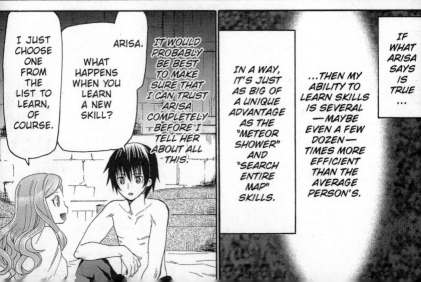

I JUST CHOOSE ONE FROM THE LIST TO LEARN, OF COURSE.

ARISA. WHAT HAPPENS WHEN YOU LEARN A NEW SKILL?

IT WOULD PROBABLY BE BEST TO MAKE SURE THAT I CAN TRUST ARISA COMPLETELY BEFORE I TELL HER ABOUT ALL THIS.

IN A WAY, IT'S JUST AS BIG OF A UNIQUE ADVANTAGE AS THE "METEOR SHOWER" AND "SEARCH ENTIRE MAP" SKILLS.

...THEN MY ABILITY TO LEARN SKILLS IS SEVERAL —MAYBE EVEN A FEW DOZEN— TIMES MORE EFFICIENT THAN THE AVERAGE PERSON'S.

IF WHAT ARISA SAYS IS TRUE...

IF YOU SATISFY CERTAIN REQUIRE-MENTS, THE NEW SKILL SHOWS UP.

WHEN MY SKILL POINTS INCREASE.

...OR A RELATED LOWER SKILL.

LIKE A CERTAIN NUMBER OF SKILL POINTS...

SO WHAT CAUSES NEW SKILLS TO APPEAR ON THE LIST?

NO, WAIT.

I FEEL LIKE I MIGHT BE MISUNDER-STANDING SOMETHING HERE.

SO THAT PART'S THE SAME...

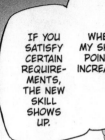

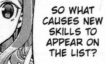

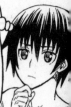

IN MY CASE, I LEARN SKILLS JUST BY PERFORMING A RELATED ACTION.

SO THAT'S DIFFERENT TOO...

YOU CAN DECIDE WHETHER TO SPEND THE POINTS NOW OR SAVE THEM FOR A BETTER SKILL.

THEY APPEAR WHEN YOU HAVE HALF OF THE REQUIRED SKILL POINTS, WHICH IS CONVENIENT.

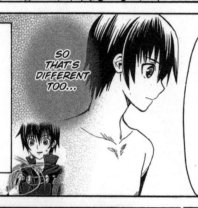

MOST IMPORTANTLY, IT LETS ME MANAGE MY STATS LIKE STR AND INT AND CHOOSE HOW TO ALLOCATE SKILL POINTS.

IT GIVES MORE INFO THAN A YAMATO STONE.

"SELF-STATUS CHECK"...

...IS JUST WHAT IT SOUNDS LIKE: A SKILL THAT LETS ME REVIEW MY OWN STATUS.

THE BEASTFOLK GIRLS SEEM TO ACQUIRE SKILLS IN A SIMILAR FASHION, SO I TRIED COMMENTING THAT THE WAY THE BEASTFOLK GIRLS ACQUIRE SKILLS SEEMS TO BE DIFFERENT FROM ARISA'S METHOD, WITHOUT MENTIONING MY OWN...

...BUT SHE SIMPLY RESPONDED THAT THERE ARE SPECIAL SYSTEMS FOR TRANS-FERENCES AND TRANSMIGRATIONS.

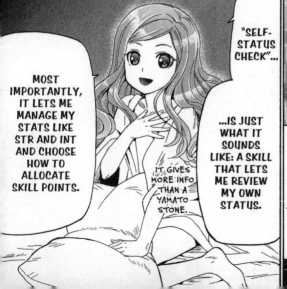

"HIDE SKILLS"...

...ALLOWS ME TO CONCEAL INFORMATION ABOUT THE SKILLS I HAVE.

ONCE IT'S BEEN USED, MY SKILLS WILL APPEAR AS 'NONE'—EVEN TO YAMATO STONES AND THE "ANALYZE" SKILL—UNTIL I DEACTIVATE IT.

BUT SHE CAN CHOOSE HOW HER ATTRIBUTES ARE ALLOTTED? MY MENU DOESN'T HAVE THAT FEATURE...

APPARENTLY, IT'S THIS "SELF-STATUS CHECK" SKILL THAT ALLOWS HER TO SELECT WHAT SKILL TO LEARN FROM A LIST WHEN SHE LEVELS UP.

I GUESS IT SHOWED UP AS "UNKNOWN" IN MY DISPLAY TOO.

INCIDENTALLY, ARISA'S "HIDE SKILLS" WAS GIVEN TO HER BY A GOD, SO EVEN PEOPLE WITH JUDGMENT-BASED SKILLS CAN'T SEE THROUGH IT, SHE SAYS.

SKILLS: Unknown

TO BE HONEST, "ANALYZE" WOULD'VE BEEN BETTER, BUT I DIDN'T HAVE ENOUGH TRANSMIGRATION BONUS POINTS.

"STATUS CHECK"...

...LETS ME VIEW THE STATUS OF OTHERS.

...IS AN ITEM-STORING SYSTEM LIKE THE KIND YOU SEE IN A LOT OF GAMES.

"ITEM BOX"...

TO TEST IT OUT, I LET HER TRY TO READ MY STATUS, BUT SHE ONLY GOT THE INFORMATION FROM MY NETWORKING PROFILE, JUST LIKE A YAMATO STONE.

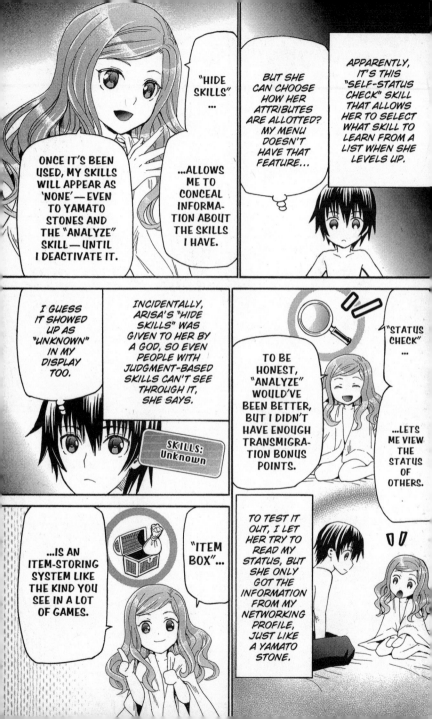

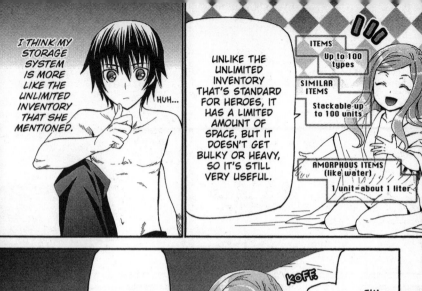

I THINK MY STORAGE SYSTEM IS MORE LIKE THE UNLIMITED INVENTORY THAT SHE MENTIONED.

HUH...

UNLIKE THE UNLIMITED INVENTORY THAT'S STANDARD FOR HEROES, IT HAS A LIMITED AMOUNT OF SPACE, BUT IT DOESN'T GET BULKY OR HEAVY, SO IT'S STILL VERY USEFUL.

ITEMS
Up to 100 types

SIMILAR ITEMS
Stackable up to 100 units

AMORPHOUS ITEMS (like water)
1 unit = about 1 liter

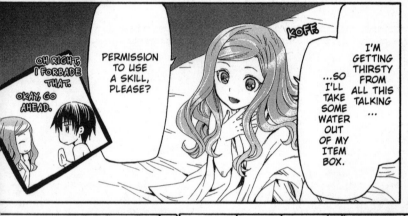

OH RIGHT, I FORBADE THAT.

OKAY, GO AHEAD.

PERMISSION TO USE A SKILL, PLEASE?

KOFF.

...SO I'LL TAKE SOME WATER OUT OF MY ITEM BOX.

I'M GETTING THIRSTY FROM ALL THIS TALKING...

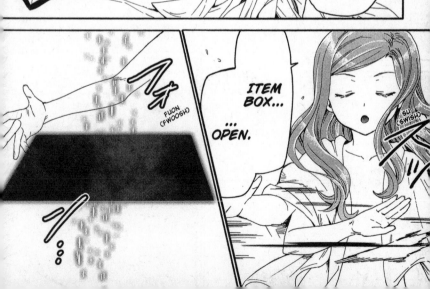

ITEM BOX... ...OPEN.

FUON (FWOOSH)

SU (SWISH)

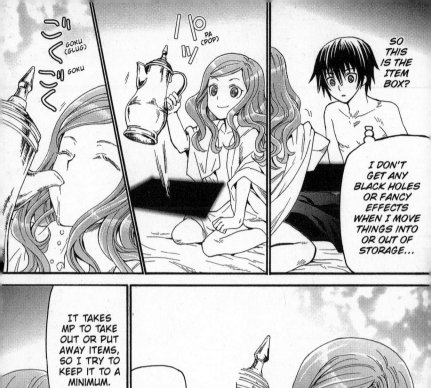

GOKU (GLUG)

GOKU

PA (POP)

SO THIS IS THE ITEM BOX?

I DON'T GET ANY BLACK HOLES OR FANCY EFFECTS WHEN I MOVE THINGS INTO OR OUT OF STORAGE...

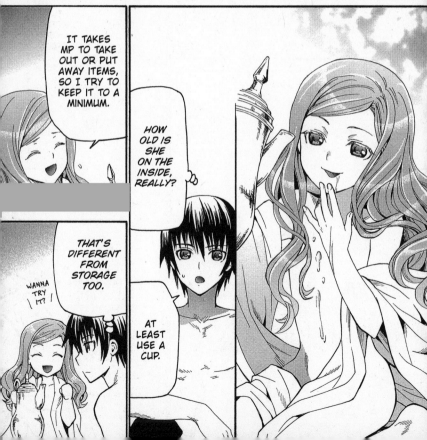

IT TAKES MP TO TAKE OUT OR PUT AWAY ITEMS, SO I TRY TO KEEP IT TO A MINIMUM.

HOW OLD IS SHE ON THE INSIDE, REALLY?

THAT'S DIFFERENT FROM STORAGE TOO.

WANNA TRY IT?

AT LEAST USE A CUP.

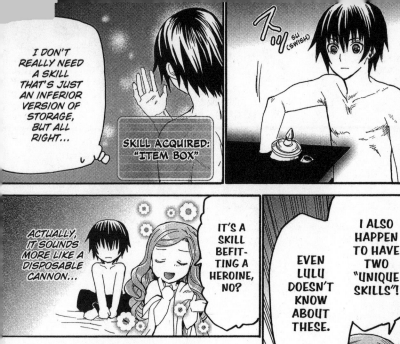

I DON'T REALLY NEED A SKILL THAT'S JUST AN INFERIOR VERSION OF STORAGE, BUT ALL RIGHT...

SKILL ACQUIRED: "ITEM BOX"

SU (SWISH)

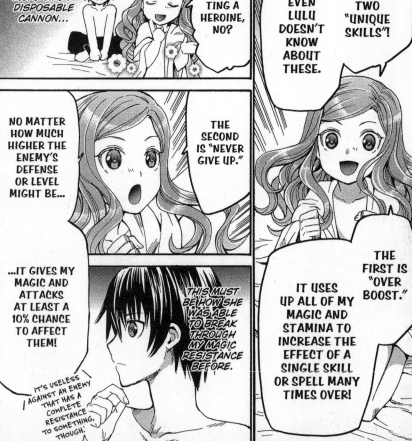

ACTUALLY, IT SOUNDS MORE LIKE A DISPOSABLE CANNON...

IT'S A SKILL BEFITTING A HEROINE, NO?

I ALSO HAPPEN TO HAVE TWO "UNIQUE SKILLS"!

EVEN LULU DOESN'T KNOW ABOUT THESE.

NO MATTER HOW MUCH HIGHER THE ENEMY'S DEFENSE OR LEVEL MIGHT BE...

THE SECOND IS "NEVER GIVE UP."

...IT GIVES MY MAGIC AND ATTACKS AT LEAST A 10% CHANCE TO AFFECT THEM!

THIS MUST BE HOW SHE WAS ABLE TO BREAK THROUGH MY MAGIC RESISTANCE BEFORE.

IT'S USELESS AGAINST AN ENEMY THAT HAS A COMPLETE RESISTANCE TO SOMETHING, THOUGH.

THE FIRST IS "OVER BOOST."

IT USES UP ALL OF MY MAGIC AND STAMINA TO INCREASE THE EFFECT OF A SINGLE SKILL OR SPELL MANY TIMES OVER!

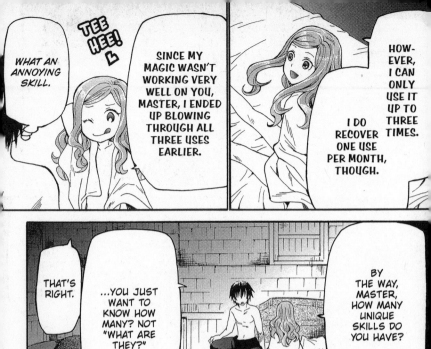

WHAT AN ANNOYING SKILL.

TEE HEE!

SINCE MY MAGIC WASN'T WORKING VERY WELL ON YOU, MASTER, I ENDED UP BLOWING THROUGH ALL THREE USES EARLIER.

HOW-EVER, I CAN ONLY USE IT UP TO THREE TIMES.

I DO RECOVER ONE USE PER MONTH, THOUGH.

THAT'S RIGHT.

...YOU JUST WANT TO KNOW HOW MANY? NOT "WHAT ARE THEY?"

BY THE WAY, MASTER, HOW MANY UNIQUE SKILLS DO YOU HAVE?

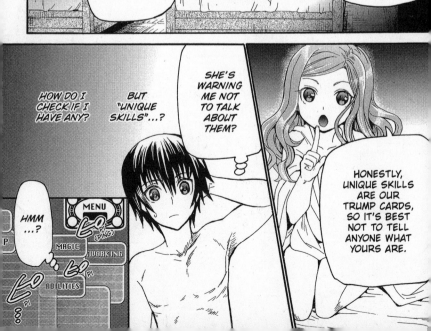

HOW DO I CHECK IF I HAVE ANY?

BUT "UNIQUE SKILLS"...?

SHE'S WARNING ME NOT TO TALK ABOUT THEM?

HMM ...?

HONESTLY, UNIQUE SKILLS ARE OUR TRUMP CARDS, SO IT'S BEST NOT TO TELL ANYONE WHAT YOURS ARE.

MENU

MAGIC

WORKING

ABILITIES

WOW!

THAT'S AMAZING!

...I HAVE FOUR.

ACCORDING TO THE GOD I MET, THE MORE SKILLS A PERSON HAS, THE GREATER THE CALIBER OF THEIR SOUL.

DOUBT THAT...

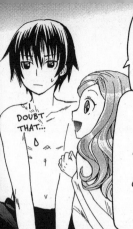

ABILITIES

PA FLASH

MENU

Unit Creation

Unit Deployment

Immortality

IT DOES SEEM TO FOLLOW A SIMILAR FRAMEWORK TO ARISA'S UNIQUE SKILLS, SO I GUESS I MIGHT AS WELL THINK OF IT THAT WAY TO KEEP THINGS FROM GETTING TOO COMPLICATED.

SO THIS MENU OF MINE IS AN ABILITY, HUH?

I GUESS MY STORAGE, RADAR, AND MAP ARE PART OF IT.

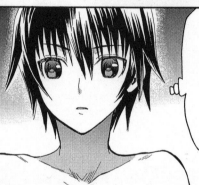

UMMM...

IT'S KIND OF A HIDDEN FEATURE OF SELF-STATUS CHECK...

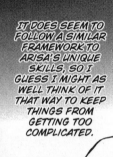

THERE ARE A FEW MORE THINGS I WANT TO KNOW.

HOW ARE YOU ABLE TO USE PSYCHIC MAGIC WITHOUT A CHANT?

I WONDER IF "IMMORTALITY" IS THE ABILITY TO REVIVE IN A CHURCH OR SOMETHING AFTER BEING KILLED, LIKE IN A GAME.

I CAN'T SELECT THE OTHER THREE.

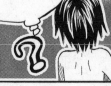

NEXT QUESTION— TELL ME WHAT YOU HAVE INSIDE YOUR ITEM BOX.

SO YOU DO HAVE TO USE THE CHANT ONCE...

I GUESS THE ONLY WAY AROUND LEARNING A DIFFICULT CHANT IS USING A MAGIC SCROLL.

ONCE I'VE LEARNED A SPELL, I ONLY HAVE TO THINK OF THE FINAL COMMAND WORD IN MY HEAD TO USE IT.

I DON'T WANT YOU PULLING OUT SOME KNIFE OR POISON OR SOMETHING AND KILLING ME IN MY SLEEP.

I HAVE A HARD TIME WITH THE CHANTS...

THAT'S NO LIE.

DOES THAT MEAN YOU CAN'T USE MAGIC, MASTER?

THERE'S ALSO THE WATER JUG I HAD BEFORE AND A FEW CHANGES OF CLOTHES.

BASA (RUSTLE)

BASA

......

LET ME SEE...

...I HAVE FIVE MAGIC BOOKS, MOSTLY ABOUT PSYCHIC MAGIC.

THEY'RE HANDMADE! I WAS GREAT AT THIS IN MY PAST LIFE.

A SAILOR SUIT AND A MAID COSTUME...

IT'S CONSIDERED AN ILL OMEN AS BOTH A HAIR COLOR AND EYE COLOR.

FEW PEOPLE KNOW WHY THAT IS, BUT WHENEVER SOMETHING BAD HAPPENS, IT'S ALWAYS BLAMED ON MY HAIR COLOR.

SO PURPLE HAIR IS A BAD OMEN?

AND IF SOMEONE WITH PURPLE HAIR LIKE MINE WERE TO PULL OUT A BOOK ON A DETESTED SUBJECT LIKE PSYCHIC MAGIC... THERE'S NO TELLING WHAT WOULD HAPPEN TO ME...

IF YOU SOLD THESE, COULDN'T YOU HAVE BOUGHT YOUR OWN FREEDOM?

IF A SLAVE HAS SUCH BELONGINGS, PEOPLE WILL SIMPLY TAKE THEM AWAY, NOT BUY THEM.

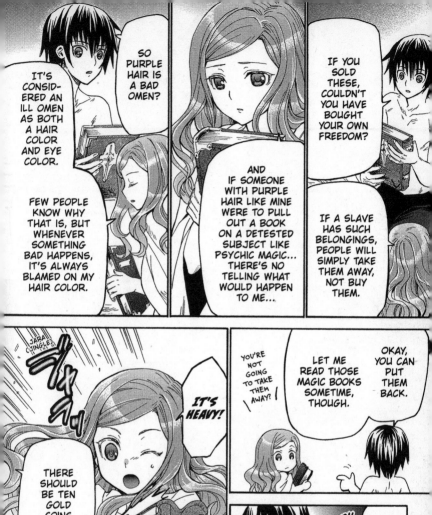

JARA! (JINGLE)

IT'S HEAVY!

THERE SHOULD BE TEN GOLD COINS IN ALL.

DON'T HESITATE TO USE THEM IF THERE'S AN EMERGENCY.

YOU'RE NOT GOING TO TAKE THEM AWAY?

LET ME READ THOSE MAGIC BOOKS SOMETIME, THOUGH.

OKAY, YOU CAN PUT THEM BACK.

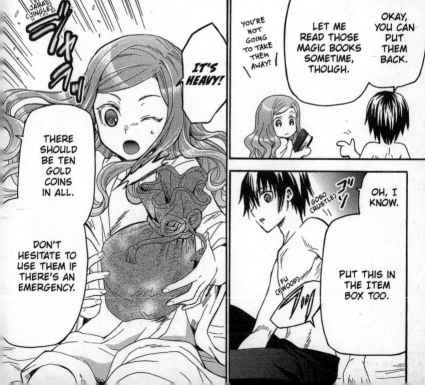

GOSO (CRUSTLE)

OH, I KNOW.

PUT THIS IN THE ITEM BOX TOO.

FU (FWOOP)

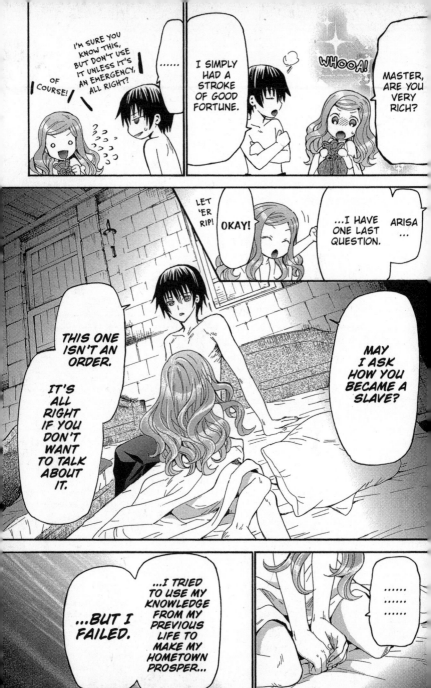

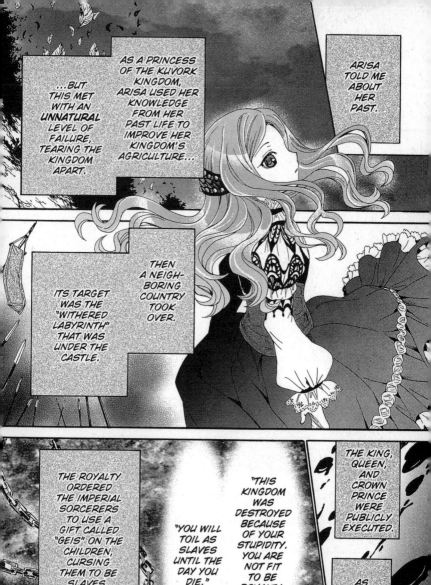

ARISA TOLD ME ABOUT HER PAST.

AS A PRINCESS OF THE KUVORK KINGDOM, ARISA USED HER KNOWLEDGE FROM HER PAST LIFE TO IMPROVE HER KINGDOM'S AGRICULTURE...

...BUT THIS MET WITH AN **UNNATURAL** LEVEL OF FAILURE, TEARING THE KINGDOM APART.

THEN A NEIGH-BORING COUNTRY TOOK OVER.

ITS TARGET WAS THE "WITHERED LABYRINTH" THAT WAS UNDER THE CASTLE.

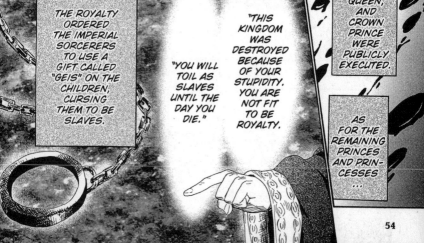

THE KING, QUEEN, AND CROWN PRINCE WERE PUBLICLY EXECUTED.

THE ROYALTY ORDERED THE IMPERIAL SORCERERS TO USE A GIFT CALLED "GEIS" ON THE CHILDREN; CURSING THEM TO BE SLAVES.

"YOU WILL TOIL AS SLAVES UNTIL THE DAY YOU DIE."

"THIS KINGDOM WAS DESTROYED BECAUSE OF YOUR STUPIDITY. YOU ARE NOT FIT TO BE ROYALTY.

AS FOR THE REMAINING PRINCES AND PRIN-CESSES...

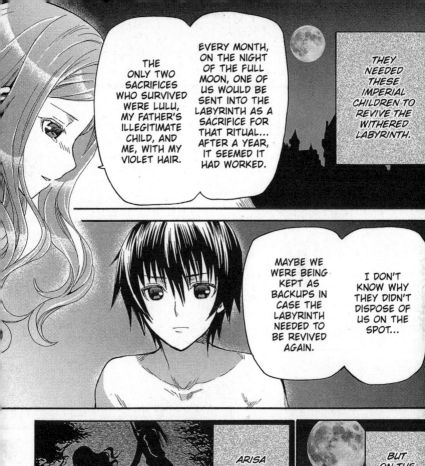

THE ONLY TWO SACRIFICES WHO SURVIVED WERE LULU, MY FATHER'S ILLEGITIMATE CHILD, AND ME, WITH MY VIOLET HAIR.

EVERY MONTH, ON THE NIGHT OF THE FULL MOON, ONE OF US WOULD BE SENT INTO THE LABYRINTH AS A SACRIFICE FOR THAT RITUAL... AFTER A YEAR, IT SEEMED IT HAD WORKED.

THEY NEEDED THESE IMPERIAL CHILDREN TO REVIVE THE WITHERED LABYRINTH.

MAYBE WE WERE BEING KEPT AS BACKUPS IN CASE THE LABYRINTH NEEDED TO BE REVIVED AGAIN.

I DON'T KNOW WHY THEY DIDN'T DISPOSE OF US ON THE SPOT...

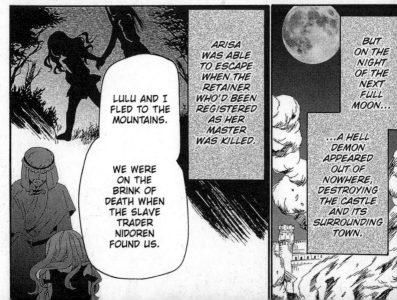

LULU AND I FLED TO THE MOUNTAINS.

WE WERE ON THE BRINK OF DEATH WHEN THE SLAVE TRADER NIDOREN FOUND US.

ARISA WAS ABLE TO ESCAPE WHEN THE RETAINER WHO'D BEEN REGISTERED AS HER MASTER WAS KILLED.

BUT ON THE NIGHT OF THE NEXT FULL MOON...

...A HELL DEMON APPEARED OUT OF NOWHERE, DESTROYING THE CASTLE AND ITS SURROUNDING TOWN.

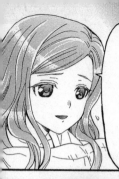

BUT I WAS SO DESPERATE TO BEHAVE PROPERLY THAT IT DIDN'T OCCUR TO ME UNTIL AFTER WE HAD GONE THROUGH WITH THE CONTRACT TO BECOME NIDOREN'S SLAVES.

YOU'RE RIGHT.

COULDN'T YOU HAVE MANIPULATED NIDOREN WITH PSYCHIC MAGIC TO TREAT YOU AS HIS DAUGHTERS OR SOMETHING LIKE THAT...?

SLAVES WITHOUT MASTERS CAN'T SIMPLY WALK INTO A TOWN, AFTER ALL.

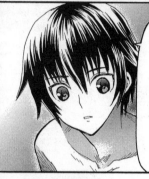

I SEE...

...BUT WHAT WAS THAT HELL DEMON'S GOAL...?

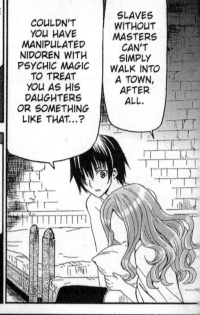

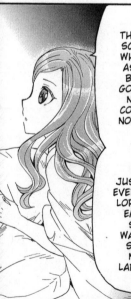

THERE ARE SCHOLARS WHO CLAIM AS MUCH, BUT THE GODS HAVE NEITHER CONFIRMED NOR DENIED IT.

STILL, JUST ABOUT EVERY DEMON LORD WHO'S EMERGED SO FAR WAS FIRST SIGHTED NEAR A LABYRINTH.

DO LABYRINTHS EXIST TO RAISE DEMON LORDS?

SINCE IT WAS A DEMON, IT WAS PROBABLY JUST LOOKING FOR A LABYRINTH TO RAISE A DEMON LORD IN, NO?

I HAVE NO IDEA.

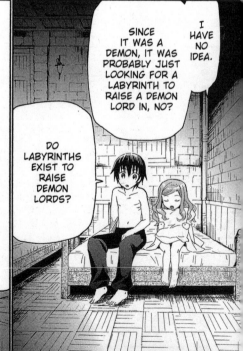

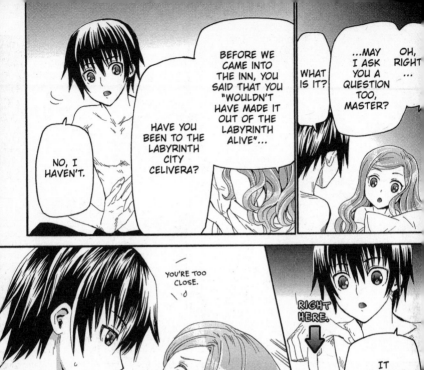

OH, RIGHT...

...MAY I ASK YOU A QUESTION TOO, MASTER?

WHAT IS IT?

BEFORE WE CAME INTO THE INN, YOU SAID THAT YOU "WOULDN'T HAVE MADE IT OUT OF THE LABYRINTH ALIVE"...

HAVE YOU BEEN TO THE LABYRINTH CITY CELIVERA?

NO, I HAVEN'T.

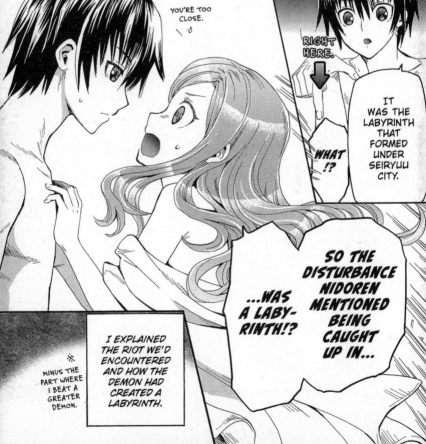

YOU'RE TOO CLOSE.

RIGHT HERE.

WHAT!?

IT WAS THE LABYRINTH THAT FORMED UNDER SEIRYUU CITY.

...WAS A LABYRINTH!?

SO THE DISTURBANCE NIDOREN MENTIONED BEING CAUGHT UP IN...

I EXPLAINED THE RIOT WE'D ENCOUNTERED AND HOW THE DEMON HAD CREATED A LABYRINTH.

※ MINUS THE PART WHERE I BEAT A GREATER DEMON.

MASS-PRODUCE MORE DEMONS AND FIGHT HEROES, MAYBE?

WHAT COULD IT HAVE BEEN TRYING TO DO...?

IS THAT REALLY SO SURPRIS-ING...?

SO YOU'RE SAYING THIS HELL DEMON CREATED A NEW LABYRINTH?

IF THAT WAS ALL, AN OLD LABYRINTH LIKE IN CELIVERA WOULD WORK JUST FINE.

THEN MAYBE IT'S JUST A DIVERSION OR PART OF SOME STRATEGY FOR THE FUTURE?

WELL, THERE ARE ONLY SIX LIVING LABYRINTHS IN THIS ENTIRE CONTINENT.

THE MOST RECENT ONE TO BE CREATED WAS MORE THAN ONE HUNDRED YEARS AGO.

THAT COULD BE THE CASE...

......
......

THERE'S WAY TOO LITTLE INFORMATION TO FIGURE OUT WHAT THE DEMON WAS THINKING OR ANYTHING LIKE THAT.

IT'S SUPPOSED TO BE IMPOSSIBLE TO CREATE A LABYRINTH WITHOUT A LEGENDARY ARTIFACT.

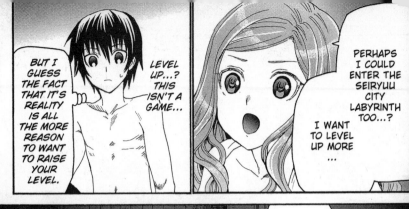

BUT I GUESS THE FACT THAT IT'S REALITY IS ALL THE MORE REASON TO WANT TO RAISE YOUR LEVEL.

LEVEL UP...? THIS ISN'T A GAME...

PERHAPS I COULD ENTER THE SEIRYUU CITY LABYRINTH TOO...?

I WANT TO LEVEL UP MORE ...

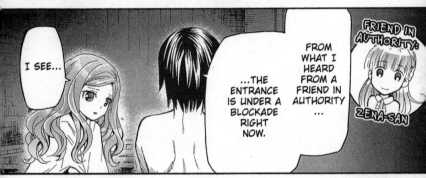

I SEE...

...THE ENTRANCE IS UNDER A BLOCKADE RIGHT NOW.

FROM WHAT I HEARD FROM A FRIEND IN AUTHORITY ...

FRIEND IN AUTHORITY:
ZENA-SAN

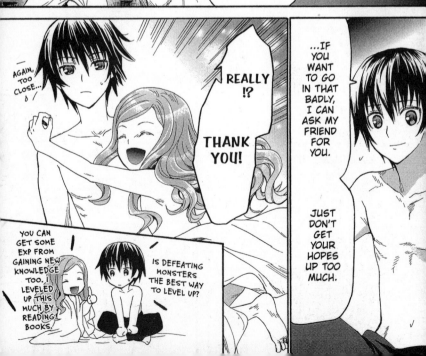

AGAIN, TOO CLOSE...

REALLY !?

THANK YOU!

...IF YOU WANT TO GO IN THAT BADLY, I CAN ASK MY FRIEND FOR YOU.

JUST DON'T GET YOUR HOPES UP TOO MUCH.

YOU CAN GET SOME EXP FROM GAINING NEW KNOWLEDGE TOO. I LEVELED UP THIS MUCH BY READING BOOKS.

IS DEFEATING MONSTERS THE BEST WAY TO LEVEL UP?

SO ARISA COULDN'T BE FREED FROM SLAVERY UNLESS THE "GEIS" WAS ERASED OR REWRITTEN WITH A SKILL.

APPARENTLY, IF SHE WENT AGAINST THE RULES OF THE "GEIS," SHE'D START BLEEDING ALL OVER AND DIE.

DOBAN
(SLAM)

...I HAD LEARNED SOME THINGS THAT MADE ME FEEL BAD FOR HER TOO, AND IT WOULD BE PRETTY HEARTLESS TO ABANDON A KID WITHOUT ANY RELATIVES IN A FOREIGN COUNTRY.

ONCE I'D FIGURED OUT THAT ARISA HAD USED MAGIC TO CHARM ME, I RESOLVED TO GET AWAY FROM HER FOR A WHILE, BUT...

MOZO
(SHIFT)

TA
(CLACK)
TA
TA
TA
KA
KA
KA
KA
(TROT)

DID I OVER-SLEEP A LITTLE...?

...I'LL JUST FOCUS ON THE PRESENT.

I MIGHT COME TO REGRET THAT KINDNESS IN THE FUTURE, BUT FOR NOW...

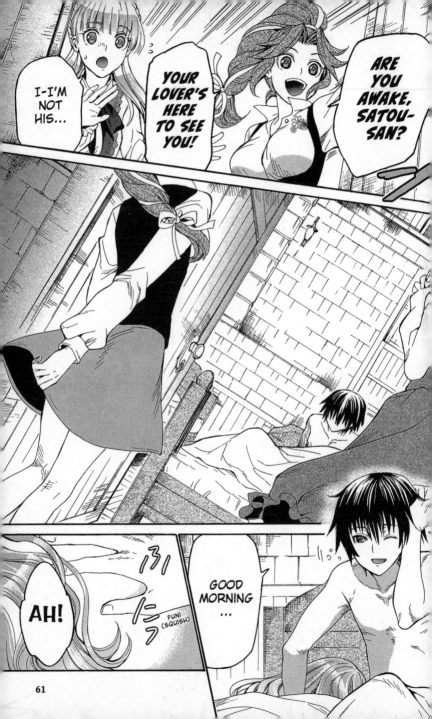

ARE YOU AWAKE, SATOU-SAN?

YOUR LOVER'S HERE TO SEE YOU!

I-I'M NOT HIS...

GOOD MORNING...

FUNI (SQUISH)

AH!

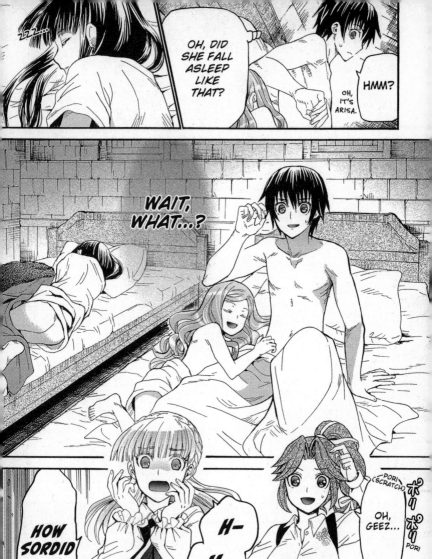

OH, DID SHE FALL ASLEEP LIKE THAT?

OH, IT'S ARISA.

HMM?

WAIT, WHAT...?

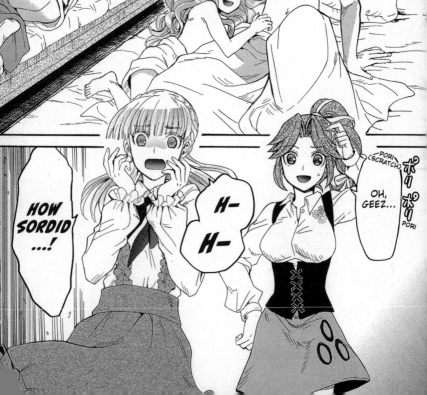

HOW SORDID ....!

H— H—

OH, GEEZ...

(SCRATCH) PORI

PORI

CHAPTER 16: MISUNDERSTANDINGS ARE THE SPICE OF LOVE

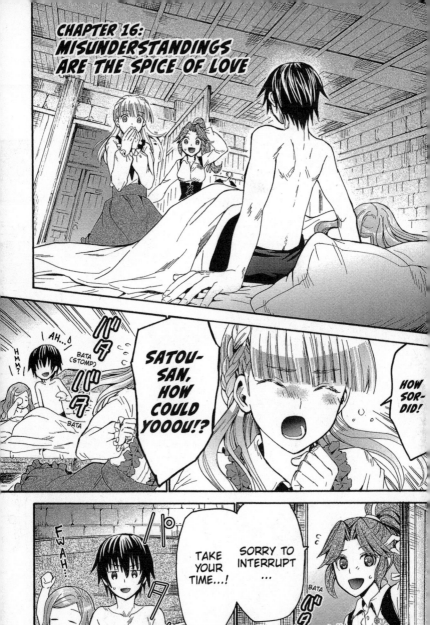

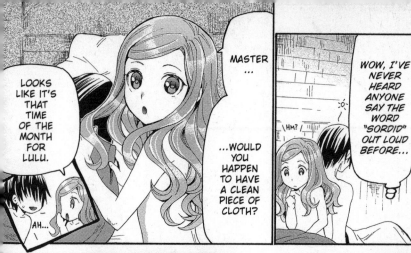
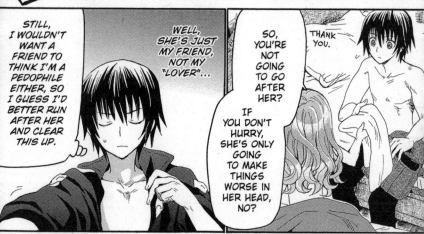
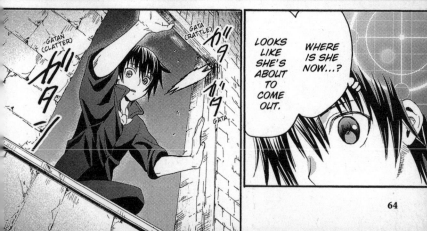

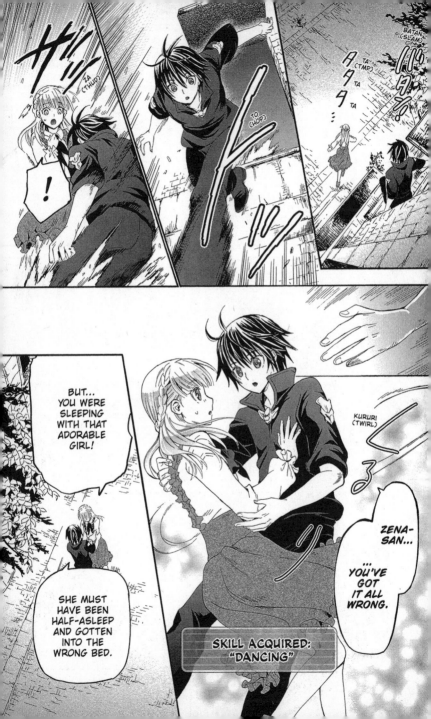

HI!!
TA (THUD)

TO (CHOP)

BATAN (SLAM)

TA (TMP)
TA
TA

BUT... YOU WERE SLEEPING WITH THAT ADORABLE GIRL!

SHE MUST HAVE BEEN HALF-ASLEEP AND GOTTEN INTO THE WRONG BED.

KURURI (TWIRL)

ZENA-SAN...

...YOU'VE GOT IT ALL WRONG.

SKILL ACQUIRED: "DANCING"

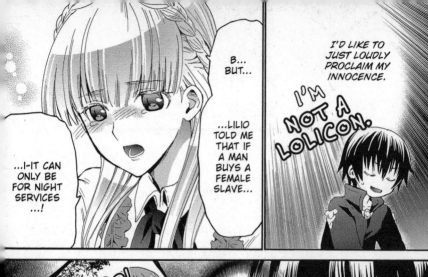

I'D LIKE TO JUST LOUDLY PROCLAIM MY INNOCENCE.

I'M NOT A LOLICON.

B... BUT...

...LILIO TOLD ME THAT IF A MAN BUYS A FEMALE SLAVE...

...I-IT CAN ONLY BE FOR NIGHT SERVICES ...!

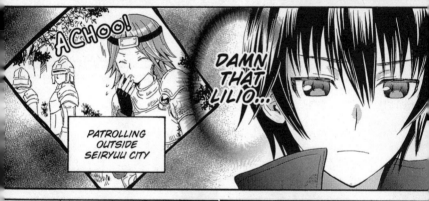

ACHOO!

DAMN THAT LILIO...

PATROLLING OUTSIDE SEIRYUU CITY

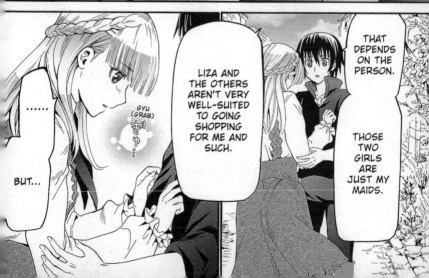

THAT DEPENDS ON THE PERSON.

LIZA AND THE OTHERS AREN'T VERY WELL-SUITED TO GOING SHOPPING FOR ME AND SUCH.

THOSE TWO GIRLS ARE JUST MY MAIDS.

......

GYU (GRAB)

BUT...

YOUR OUTFIT TODAY MAKES YOU LOOK VERY DIFFERENT FROM LAST TIME.

HUH?

THE FRILLS ADD A NICE TOUCH OF FLASHINESS TO YOUR CLASSIC NEAT AND TIDY LOOK...

IT REALLY DRAWS OUT YOUR CHARMS.

OPERATION VAGUE COMPLIMENTS

OH... THIS OLD THING...

IT'S LOVELY, BUT AREN'T YOU COLD BEING SO LIGHTLY DRESSED?

MOJI
MOJI
[MOJI [FIDGET]]

NO, I'M QUITE USED TO IT, SO I'M FINE.

THAT'S NOT HOW THAT EXCHANGE IS SUPPOSED TO GO, ZENA-SAN.

REALLY? I'D LOVE TO SEE!

PAA [SHINE]

WOULD YOU LIKE TO GO TAKE A LOOK? I'M SURE THEY'D LOOK GREAT ON YOU, ZENA-SAN.

OH, RIGHT!

THERE'S A STALL NEAR HERE THAT SELLS SOME BEAUTIFUL SCARVES.

...BUT BY THE TIME WE LEFT THE STORE, SHE SEEMED TO BE COMPLETELY BACK TO NORMAL.

IT TOOK A LITTLE BIT OF ARGUING TO GET HER TO ACCEPT IT...

...ZENA-SAN PICKED OUT A PINK SCARF, AND I BOUGHT IT FOR HER AS A PRESENT.

AFTER WE INSPECTED DOZENS UPON DOZENS OF SCARVES AND SHAWLS...

YES! I MANAGED TO CHANGE THE SUBJECT!

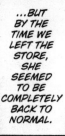

PHEW!

PLEASE, GO AHEAD.

OH, I CAN'T ACCEPT THIS!

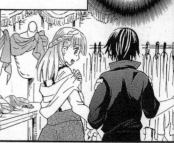

AH!

ヂ
ヂ
ヂ
GASA (RUSTLE)

ヂ
GASA

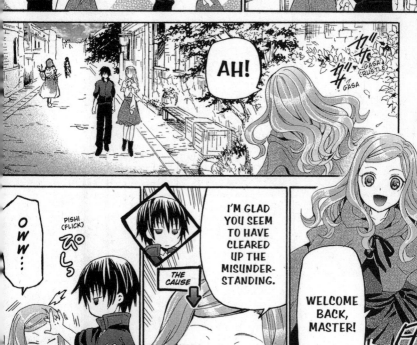

O W W...

PISHI (FLICK)

THE CAUSE

I'M GLAD YOU SEEM TO HAVE CLEARED UP THE MISUNDERSTANDING.

WELCOME BACK, MASTER!

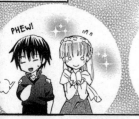

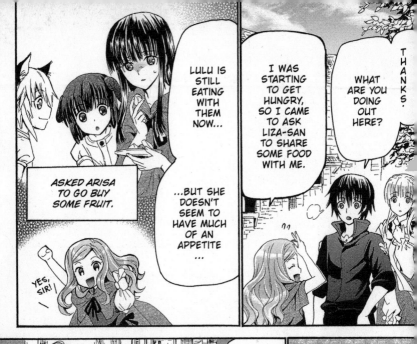

LULU IS STILL EATING WITH THEM NOW...

...BUT SHE DOESN'T SEEM TO HAVE MUCH OF AN APPETITE...

ASKED ARISA TO GO BUY SOME FRUIT.

YES, SIR!

I WAS STARTING TO GET HUNGRY, SO I CAME TO ASK LIZA-SAN TO SHARE SOME FOOD WITH ME.

WHAT ARE YOU DOING OUT HERE?

THANKS.

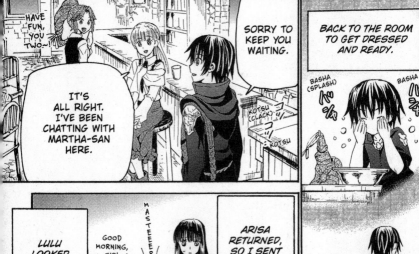

HAVE FUN, YOU TWO~

SORRY TO KEEP YOU WAITING.

IT'S ALL RIGHT. I'VE BEEN CHATTING WITH MARTHA-SAN HERE.

KOTSU (CLACK)

KOTSU

BACK TO THE ROOM TO GET DRESSED AND READY.

BASHA (SPLASH)

BASHA

LULU LOOKED AWFULLY PALE, SO I LET HER RETURN TO THE ROOM.

GOOD MORNING, SIR!

MASTEEEER?

ARISA RETURNED, SO I SENT HER TO SUMMON LIZA AND THE OTHERS.

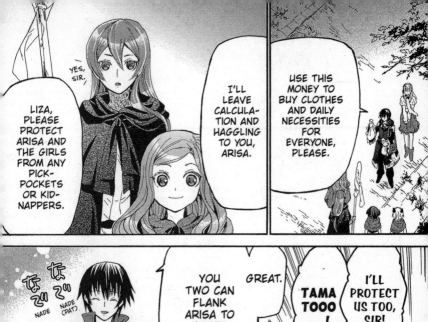

LIZA, PLEASE PROTECT ARISA AND THE GIRLS FROM ANY PICK-POCKETS OR KID-NAPPERS.

YES, SIR.

I'LL LEAVE CALCULATION AND HAGGLING TO YOU, ARISA.

USE THIS MONEY TO BUY CLOTHES AND DAILY NECESSITIES FOR EVERYONE, PLEASE.

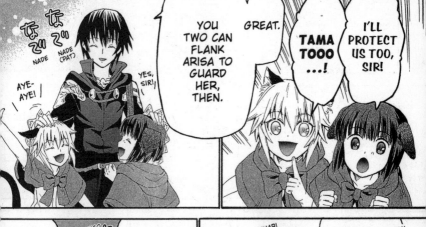

NADE NADE (PAT)

AYE-AYE!

YES, SIR!

YOU TWO CAN FLANK ARISA TO GUARD HER, THEN.

GREAT.

TAMA TOOO...!

I'LL PROTECT US TOO, SIR!

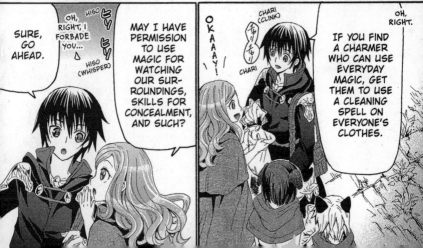

SURE, GO AHEAD.

HISO HISO (WHISPER)

OH, RIGHT, I FORBADE YOU...

MAY I HAVE PERMISSION TO USE MAGIC FOR WATCHING OUR SURROUNDINGS, SKILLS FOR CONCEALMENT, AND SUCH?

OKAAAY!

CHARI (CLINK)

CHARI

OH, RIGHT.

IF YOU FIND A CHARMER WHO CAN USE EVERYDAY MAGIC, GET THEM TO USE A CLEANING SPELL ON EVERYONE'S CLOTHES.

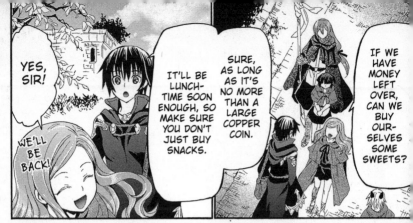

YES, SIR!

WE'LL BE BACK!

IT'LL BE LUNCH-TIME SOON ENOUGH, SO MAKE SURE YOU DON'T JUST BUY SNACKS.

SURE, AS LONG AS IT'S NO MORE THAN A LARGE COPPER COIN.

IF WE HAVE MONEY LEFT OVER, CAN WE BUY OUR-SELVES SOME SWEETS?

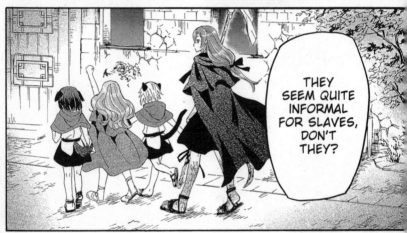

THEY SEEM QUITE INFORMAL FOR SLAVES, DON'T THEY?

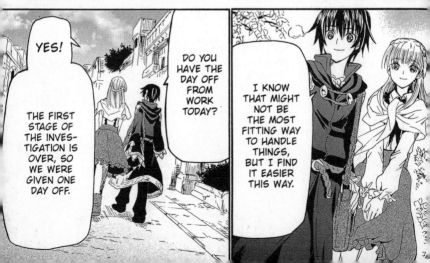

YES!

THE FIRST STAGE OF THE INVES-TIGATION IS OVER, SO WE WERE GIVEN ONE DAY OFF.

DO YOU HAVE THE DAY OFF FROM WORK TODAY?

I KNOW THAT MIGHT NOT BE THE MOST FITTING WAY TO HANDLE THINGS, BUT I FIND IT EASIER THIS WAY.

ONCE SHE REJOINS HER UNIT, I PROBABLY WON'T BE ABLE TO SEE HER MUCH.

UNITS WITH MAGIC SOLDIERS GO OUT ON LONGER PATROL ROUTES, SO...

I WON'T BE ABLE TO GO BACK TO MY USUAL PATROL FOR AT LEAST FIVE MORE DAYS.

NO, A NEWLY ESTABLISHED SPECIAL LABYRINTH FORCE WILL BE TAKING OVER STARTING TOMORROW.

WILL YOU BE GOING BACK TO YOUR HOME UNIT TOMORROW?

NO, NO, IT'S NOTHING LIKE THAT.

IS THERE SOMEONE YOU KNOW WHO STILL HASN'T COME OUT OF THE LABYRINTH?

I'M SORRY IF I WORRIED YOU.

YES...

...IT WILL PROBABLY STAY CLOSED FOR SEVERAL MONTHS AT LEAST.

ZENA-SAN, IS THE LABYRINTH CLOSED TO EVERYONE BUT MILITARY PERSONNEL RIGHT NOW?

COME TO THINK OF IT, DIDN'T ARISA WANT TO GO INTO THE LABYRINTH?

OZU (FRET)

DO YOU HAVE ANY PLANS FOR TODAY...?

SATOU-SAN...

IT'LL BE A LITTLE SAD TO SAY GOOD-BYE TO ZENA-SAN, BUT I'M SURE I CAN COME BACK AND VISIT AGAIN.

MAYBE WE SHOULD HEAD TO LABYRINTH CITY WHEN WE'RE DONE SIGHTSEEING IN SEIRYUU CITY?

LOOKS LIKE ARISA WON'T BE GETTING HER WISH ANYTIME SOON.

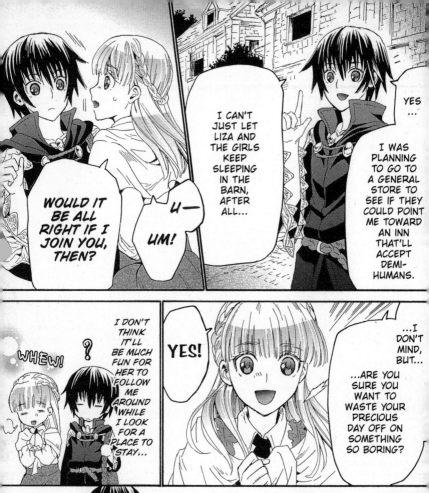

WOULD IT BE ALL RIGHT IF I JOIN YOU, THEN?

U— UM!

I CAN'T JUST LET LIZA AND THE GIRLS KEEP SLEEPING IN THE BARN, AFTER ALL...

YES...

I WAS PLANNING TO GO TO A GENERAL STORE TO SEE IF THEY COULD POINT ME TOWARD AN INN THAT'LL ACCEPT DEMI-HUMANS.

I DON'T THINK IT'LL BE MUCH FUN FOR HER TO FOLLOW ME AROUND WHILE I LOOK FOR A PLACE TO STAY...

WHEW!

YES!

...I DON'T MIND, BUT...

...ARE YOU SURE YOU WANT TO WASTE YOUR PRECIOUS DAY OFF ON SOMETHING SO BORING?

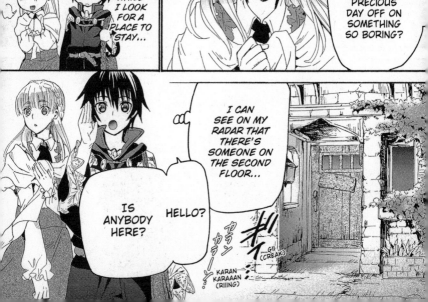

I CAN SEE ON MY RADAR THAT THERE'S SOMEONE ON THE SECOND FLOOR...

IS ANYBODY HERE?

HELLO?

カラン カラー

GII (CREAK)

KARAN KARAAAN (RIIING)

WELL...

...I WAS HOPING YOU'D BE ABLE TO RECOMMEND ME A GOOD INN OR A HOUSE FOR RENT.

HOW CAN I HELP YOU?

KATSUN (STROMP)

KATSU

COMING!

WITH DEMI-HUMANS, YOU'LL BE BEST OFF IN THE WEST QUARTER OR THE NEARBY WORKERS' DISTRICT.

TERMS

* ALLOWS DEMI-HUMAN SLAVES

* GOOD SECURITY

GASA GASA (SHUFFLE)

THANK YOU FOR WAITING.

I'D BE WORRIED ABOUT THE CHANCES OF CRIME AT AN INN IN THE WEST QUARTER, SO I THINK A RENTED HOUSE WOULD BE IDEAL.

PARA (FLIP)

PARA

I'M NADI, A GENERAL MERCHANT.

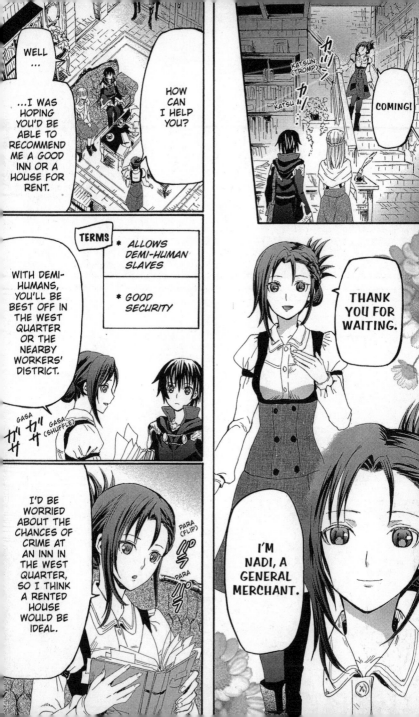

APPARENTLY, ALL THREE OF THESE HOUSES HAD A QUESTIONABLE HISTORY.

HOW-EVER...

IN THAT CASE, I BELIEVE THAT THESE THREE PLACES WOULD BE ABLE TO MEET YOUR REQUESTS.

AROUND THIS MUCH...

AND YOUR BUDGET?

KASA (RUSTLE)

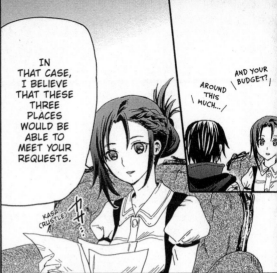

DIRECTLY BEHIND A STREET LINED WITH BROTHELS.

HOUSE TWO

HOO-HOO!

KAAAA (BLUSHHH)

......

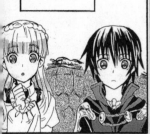

HOUSE ONE

I DECIDED IT WOULD BE BEST TO HAVE A LOOK AT EACH.

THE PREVIOUS OWNER WAS ASSASSINATED BY A MEMBER OF SOME CRIMINAL GUILD.

BUT THIS PLACE HAS...

HOUSE THREE

A DILAPIDATED MANSION SAID TO BE HAUNTED BY GHOSTS.

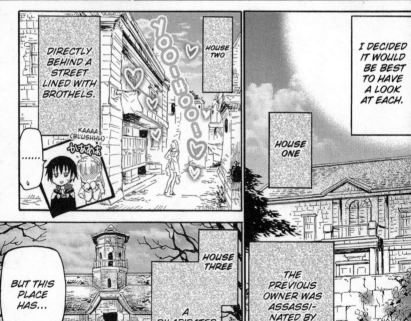

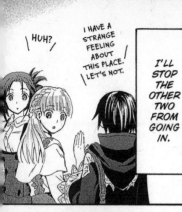

HUH?

I HAVE A STRANGE FEELING ABOUT THIS PLACE. LET'S NOT.

I'LL STOP THE OTHER TWO FROM GOING IN.

THERE'S AN UNDER-GROUND TUNNEL OUT OF THE CITY...

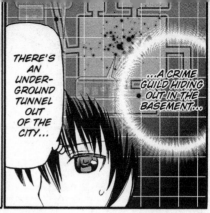

...A CRIME GUILD HIDING OUT IN THE BASEMENT...

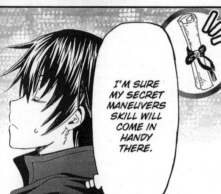

I'M SURE MY SECRET MANEUVERS SKILL WILL COME IN HANDY THERE.

I'LL JUST WRITE A LETTER LATER EXPLAINING WHAT I KNOW AND DROP IT OFF AT A GUARD STATION OR SOMETHING.

IF THERE'RE UNDEAD HERE, YOU COULD ALWAYS PAY A TEMPLE TO COME AND DO AN EXORCISM.

FORGET IT, FORGET IT.

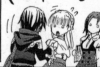

*1 TRIMOON = 10 DAYS

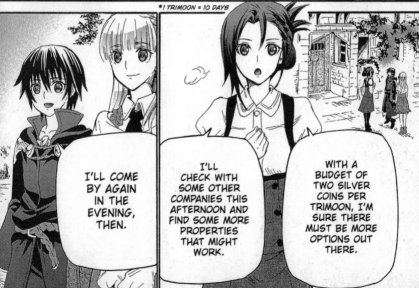

I'LL COME BY AGAIN IN THE EVENING, THEN.

I'LL CHECK WITH SOME OTHER COMPANIES THIS AFTERNOON AND FIND SOME MORE PROPERTIES THAT MIGHT WORK.

WITH A BUDGET OF TWO SILVER COINS PER TRIMOON, I'M SURE THERE MUST BE MORE OPTIONS OUT THERE.

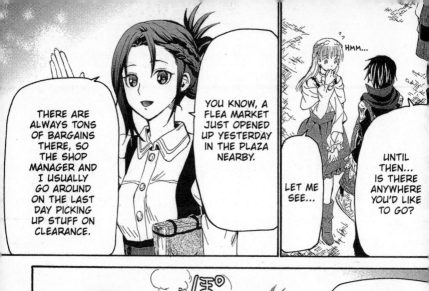

THERE ARE ALWAYS TONS OF BARGAINS THERE, SO THE SHOP MANAGER AND I USUALLY GO AROUND ON THE LAST DAY PICKING UP STUFF ON CLEARANCE.

YOU KNOW, A FLEA MARKET JUST OPENED UP YESTERDAY IN THE PLAZA NEARBY.

HMM...

LET ME SEE...

UNTIL THEN... IS THERE ANYWHERE YOU'D LIKE TO GO?

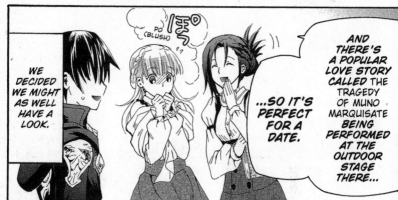

PO (BLUSH)

WE DECIDED WE MIGHT AS WELL HAVE A LOOK.

...SO IT'S PERFECT FOR A DATE.

AND THERE'S A POPULAR LOVE STORY CALLED THE TRAGEDY OF MUNO MARQUISATE BEING PERFORMED AT THE OUTDOOR STAGE THERE...

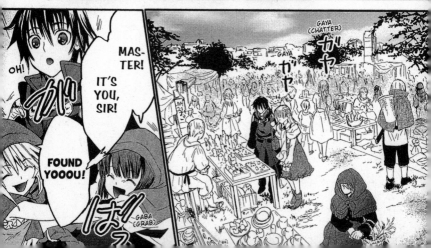

OH!

MASTER!

IT'S YOU, SIR!

FOUND YOOOU!

GABA (GRAB)

GAYA (CHATTER)

GAYA

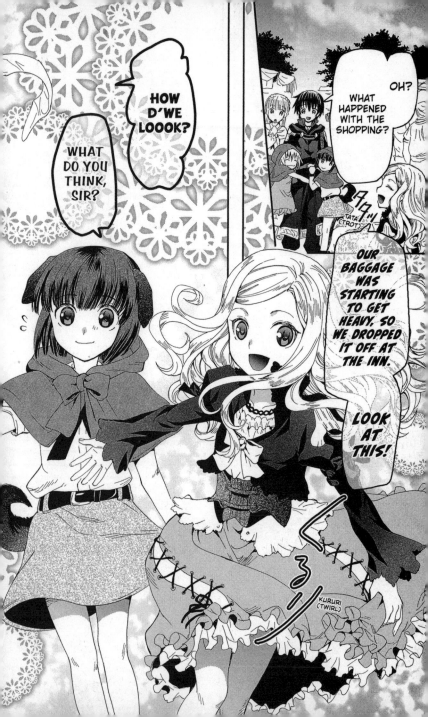

NOW,
NOW.

KURU
(SPIN)
くる

くる

YOU ALL LOOK VERY CUTE.

SINCE MY REAL HAIR COLOR'S CURSED.

EH HEH HEH~!

BY THE WAY, IS THAT A WIG?

THAT'S OKAY, RIGHT?

むぎゅっ
MUGYU (TUG)

BUT...

...THERE IS ONE MORE THING THAT I WANTED TO TALK TO YOU ABOUT BUYING...

じとーっ
JITO (GLOWER)

CUT IT OUT.

?

WHAT IS IT YOU NEED?

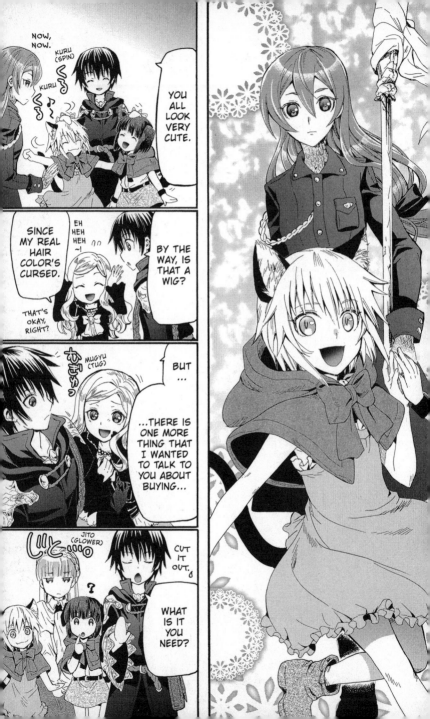

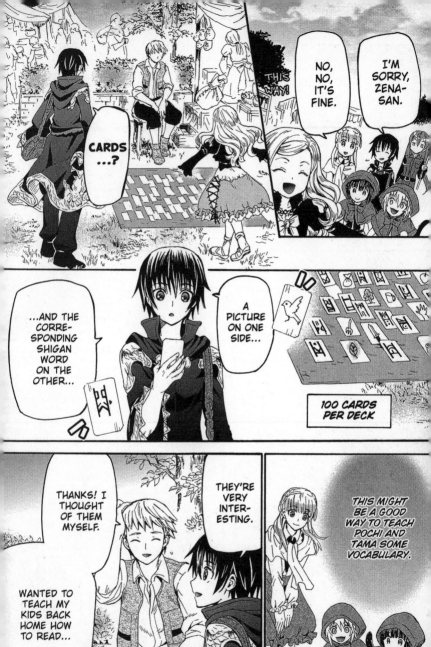

CARDS...?

THIS WAY!

NO, NO, IT'S FINE.

I'M SORRY, ZENA-SAN.

...AND THE CORRESPONDING SHIGAN WORD ON THE OTHER...

A PICTURE ON ONE SIDE...

100 CARDS PER DECK

THANKS! I THOUGHT OF THEM MYSELF.

THEY'RE VERY INTERESTING.

WANTED TO TEACH MY KIDS BACK HOME HOW TO READ...

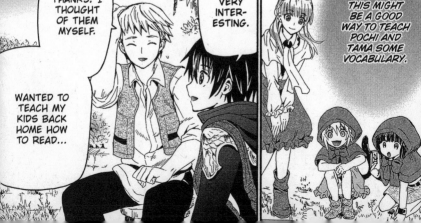

THIS MIGHT BE A GOOD WAY TO TEACH POCHI AND TAMA SOME VOCABULARY.

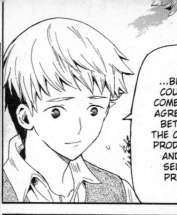

WHY DON'T Y—?

!

WOULDN'T IT BE MUCH CHEAPER TO USE WOOD-BLOCK PRINTS?

...BUT WE COULDN'T COME TO AN AGREEMENT BETWEEN THE COST OF PRODUCTION AND THE SELLING PRICE...

I TRIED TO FIND A COMPANY TO SELL THEM...

GUI (GRAB)

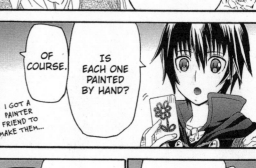

OF COURSE.

IS EACH ONE PAINTED BY HAND?

I GOT A PAINTER FRIEND TO MAKE THEM...

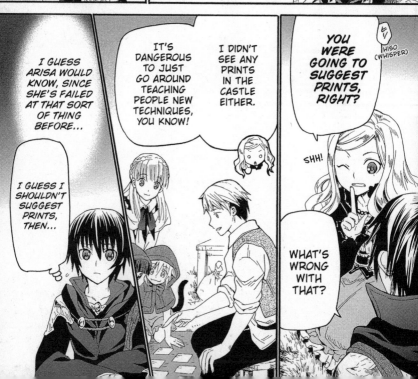

I GUESS ARISA WOULD KNOW, SINCE SHE'S FAILED AT THAT SORT OF THING BEFORE...

IT'S DANGEROUS TO JUST GO AROUND TEACHING PEOPLE NEW TECHNIQUES, YOU KNOW!

I DIDN'T SEE ANY PRINTS IN THE CASTLE EITHER.

YOU WERE GOING TO SUGGEST PRINTS, RIGHT?

HISO (WHISPER)

I GUESS I SHOULDN'T SUGGEST PRINTS, THEN...

SHH!

WHAT'S WRONG WITH THAT?

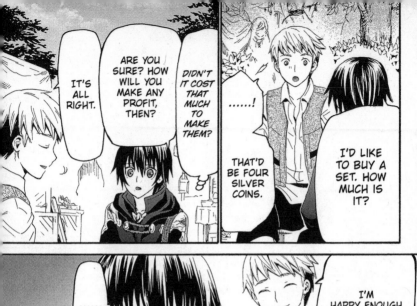

IT'S ALL RIGHT.

ARE YOU SURE? HOW WILL YOU MAKE ANY PROFIT, THEN?

DIDN'T IT COST THAT MUCH TO MAKE THEM?

......!

THAT'D BE FOUR SILVER COINS.

I'D LIKE TO BUY A SET. HOW MUCH IS IT?

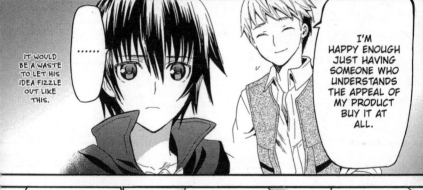

IT WOULD BE A WASTE TO LET HIS IDEA FIZZLE OUT LIKE THIS.

......

I'M HAPPY ENOUGH JUST HAVING SOMEONE WHO UNDERSTANDS THE APPEAL OF MY PRODUCT BUY IT AT ALL.

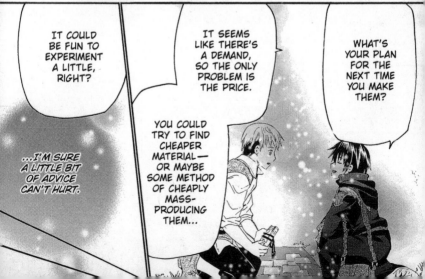

IT COULD BE FUN TO EXPERIMENT A LITTLE, RIGHT?

IT SEEMS LIKE THERE'S A DEMAND, SO THE ONLY PROBLEM IS THE PRICE.

WHAT'S YOUR PLAN FOR THE NEXT TIME YOU MAKE THEM?

YOU COULD TRY TO FIND CHEAPER MATERIAL— OR MAYBE SOME METHOD OF CHEAPLY MASS-PRODUCING THEM...

...I'M SURE A LITTLE BIT OF ADVICE CAN'T HURT.

YOU COULD DO THAT, BUT THEN YOU'D HAVE TO STAND IN THE BACK AND WATCH.

A FRIEND TOLD ME IT ONLY COSTS A SMALL COIN IF YOU PAY AT THE STAGE ENTRANCE...

THE TICKETS COST TWO COPPER COINS, BUT YOU CAN GET A SEAT INSIDE IF YOU HAVE THEM.

MASTER, AREN'T YOU GOING TO SEE THE STAGE PLAY?

THAT'S THE PLAN.

YOU BOUGHT THE TICKETS THEY WERE SELLING AT THE ENTRANCE TO THE FLEA MARKET, THEN?

NO, I DIDN'T...

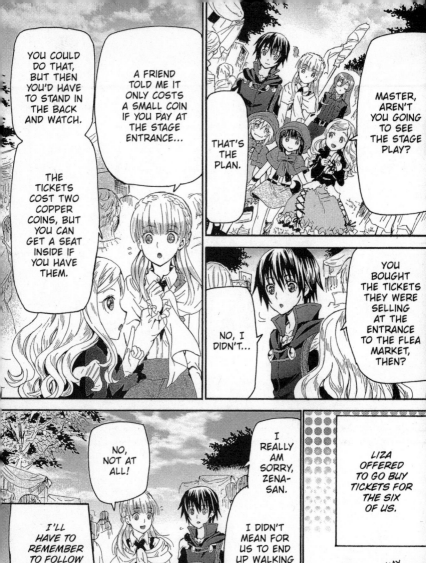

NO, NOT AT ALL!

I REALLY AM SORRY, ZENA-SAN.

I DIDN'T MEAN FOR US TO END UP WALKING AROUND WITH MY GROUP...

I'LL HAVE TO REMEMBER TO FOLLOW UP WITH HER ABOUT THIS LATER...

LIZA OFFERED TO GO BUY TICKETS FOR THE SIX OF US.

LEAVE IT TO ME.

OKAY, HERE'S THE MONEY!

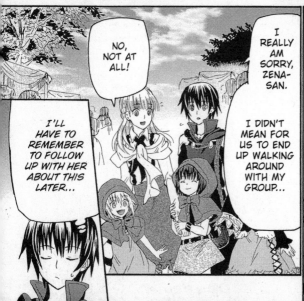

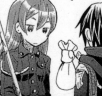

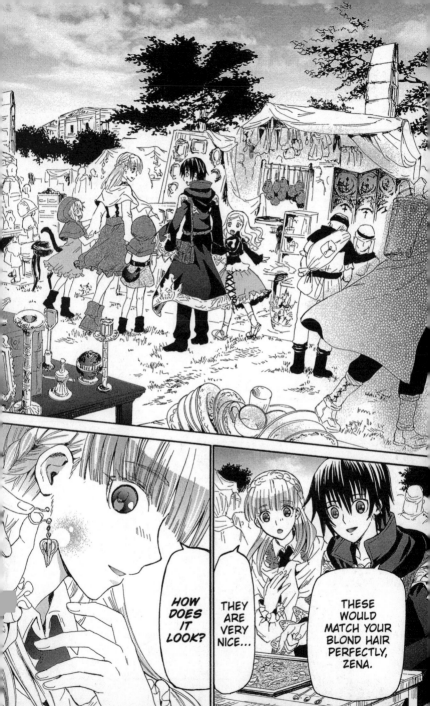

HOW DOES IT LOOK?

THEY ARE VERY NICE...

THESE WOULD MATCH YOUR BLOND HAIR PERFECTLY, ZENA.

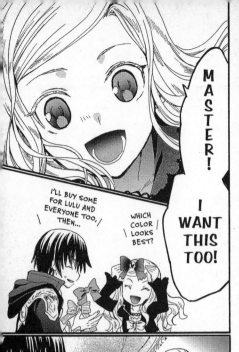

MASTER! I WANT THIS TOO!

I'LL BUY SOME FOR LULU AND EVERYONE TOO, THEN...

WHICH COLOR LOOKS BEST?

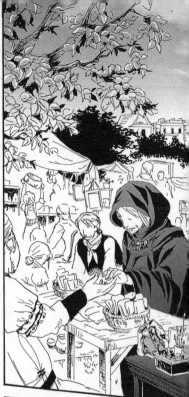

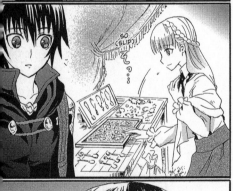

SO (SLIP)

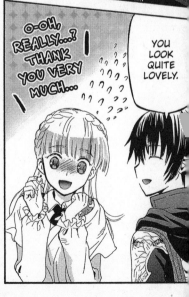

O-OH, REALLY...? THANK YOU VERY MUCH...

YOU LOOK QUITE LOVELY.

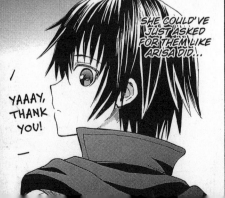

SHE COULD'VE JUST ASKED FOR THEM LIKE ARISA DID...

YAAAY, THANK YOU!

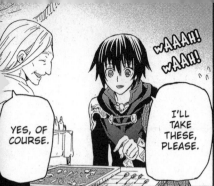

YES, OF COURSE.

WAAAH! WAAH!

I'LL TAKE THESE, PLEASE.

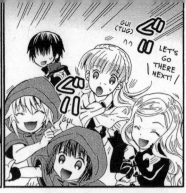

GUI (TUG)

LET'S GO THERE NEXT!

GUI

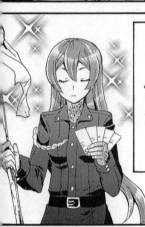

BEFORE LONG, WE MET UP WITH LIZA, WHO'D BOUGHT THE TICKETS FOR US.

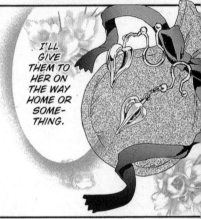

I'LL GIVE THEM TO HER ON THE WAY HOME OR SOMETHING.

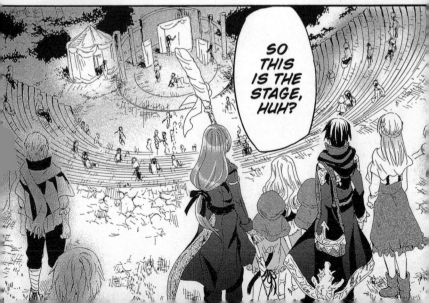

SO THIS IS THE STAGE, HUH?

A TRAGIC ROMANTIC PLAY BASED ON A TRUE STORY.

THE TRAGEDY OF MUNO MARQUISATE...

CHAPTER 17: THEATERGOING

SUUUP!!! (SNOOZE)

POCHI AND TAMA COULDN'T KEEP UP WITH THE STORY.

...AND THAT WOMAN IS THE HEROINE?

SO THE ACTOR IN THE ROBE IS THE HERO...

AS A RESULT, THE CHARACTERS ARE RATHER CONFUSING.

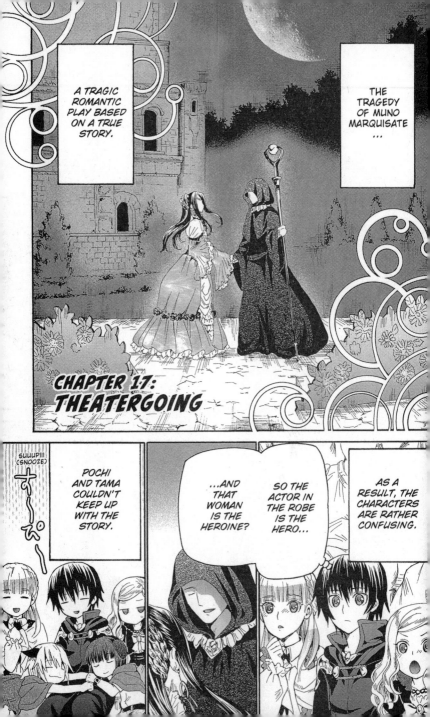

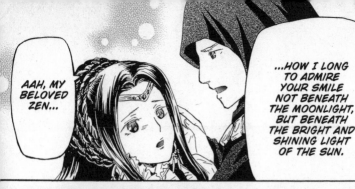

AAH, MY BELOVED ZEN...

...HOW I LONG TO ADMIRE YOUR SMILE NOT BENEATH THE MOONLIGHT, BUT BENEATH THE BRIGHT AND SHINING LIGHT OF THE SUN.

MY BEAUTIFUL MAIDEN LILTIENA...

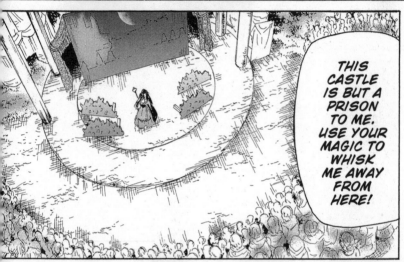

THIS CASTLE IS BUT A PRISON TO ME. USE YOUR MAGIC TO WHISK ME AWAY FROM HERE!

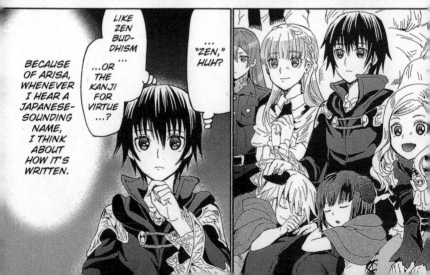

BECAUSE OF ARISA, WHENEVER I HEAR A JAPANESE-SOUNDING NAME, I THINK ABOUT HOW IT'S WRITTEN.

LIKE ZEN BUD-DHISM...

...OR THE KANJI FOR VIRTUE...?

..."ZEN," HUH?

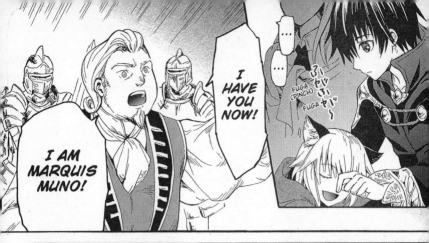

I HAVE YOU NOW!

I AM MARQUIS MUNO!

...

...

FUGA (PINCH!)
FUGA (PINCH!)

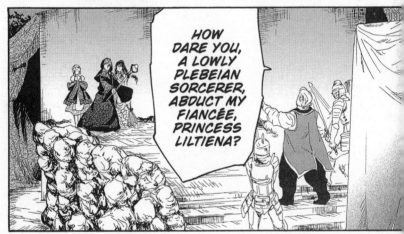

HOW DARE YOU, A LOWLY PLEBEIAN SORCERER, ABDUCT MY FIANCÊE, PRINCESS LILTIENA?

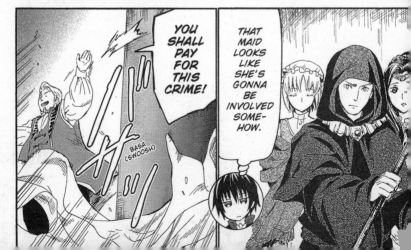

YOU SHALL PAY FOR THIS CRIME!

THAT MAID LOOKS LIKE SHE'S GONNA BE INVOLVED SOMEHOW.

BASA (SWOOSH)

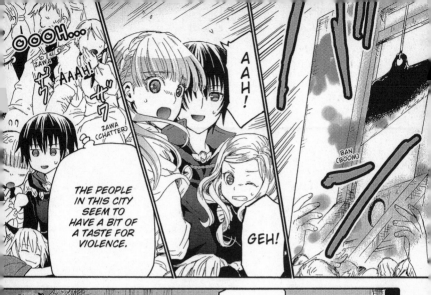

OOOH...

ZAWA

AAAH!

ZAWA (CHATTER)

AAH!

THE PEOPLE IN THIS CITY SEEM TO HAVE A BIT OF A TASTE FOR VIOLENCE.

GEH!

BAN (BOOM)

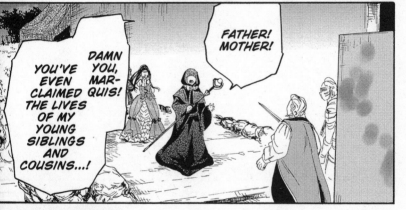

DAMN YOU, MAR-QUIS!

YOU'VE EVEN CLAIMED THE LIVES OF MY YOUNG SIBLINGS AND COUSINS...!

FATHER! MOTHER!

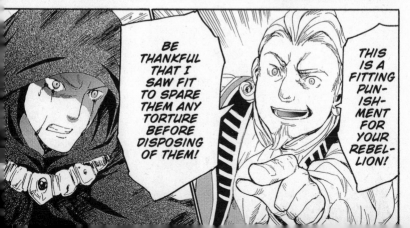

BE THANKFUL THAT I SAW FIT TO SPARE THEM ANY TORTURE BEFORE DISPOSING OF THEM!

THIS IS A FITTING PUN-ISH-MENT FOR YOUR REBEL-LION!

OOOOOOO
(WHOOOOSH)

AAAH!

SINCE
THERE
ARE
REAL
SOR-
CERERS
IN THIS
WORLD
AND
ALL...

...MAKES
SENSE
THEY
USE
REAL
MAGIC
IN THE
PERFOR-
MANCE...

WAAH!

SULU
(RUSTLE)

THERE IS
NO ONE
LEFT TO
PROTECT
YOU.

I WILL
NOW
TAKE MY
REVENGE
FOR MY
FAMILY!

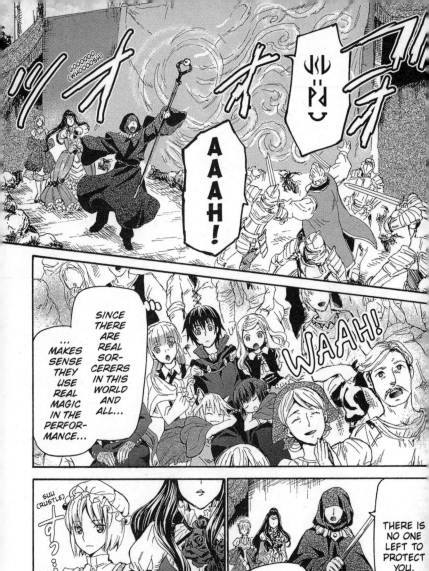

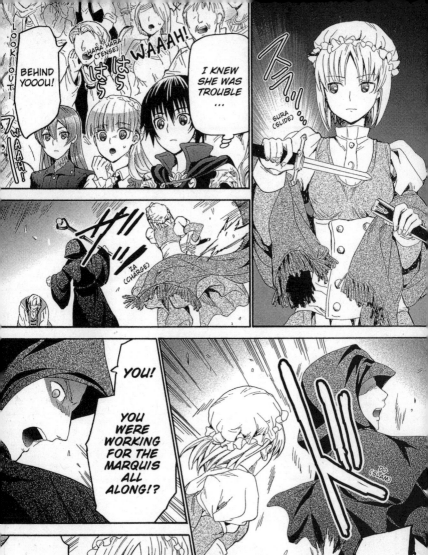

LOOK OUT! BEHIND YOOOU!

HARA HARA (TENSE)

WAAAH!

I KNEW SHE WAS TROUBLE...

SURA (SLIDE)

ZA (CHARGE)

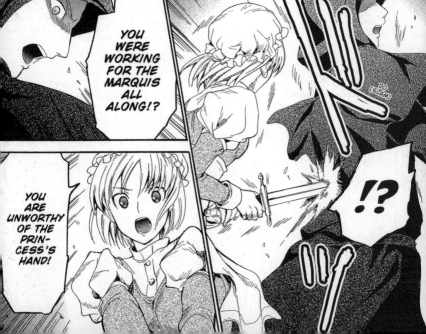

YOU!

YOU WERE WORKING FOR THE MARQUIS ALL ALONG!?

DO (SLAM)

!?

YOU ARE UNWORTHY OF THE PRINCESS'S HAND!

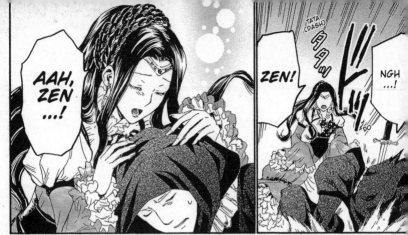

AAH, ZEN ...!

ZEN!

NGH ...!

TATA (DASH)

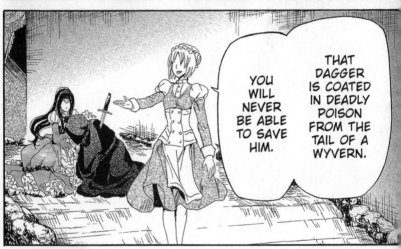

THAT DAGGER IS COATED IN DEADLY POISON FROM THE TAIL OF A WYVERN.

YOU WILL NEVER BE ABLE TO SAVE HIM.

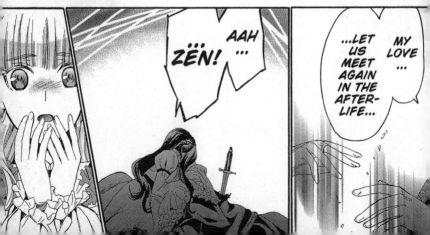

ZËN! ...

AAH ...

...LET US MEET AGAIN IN THE AFTER-LIFE...

MY LOVE ...

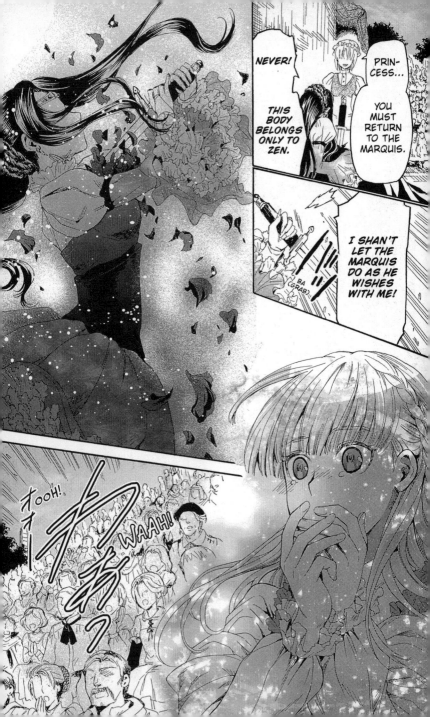

I THOUGHT IT WOULD END THERE...

...BUT THE PLAY KEPT GOING.

I DID HEAR THAT THIS WAS A TRAGIC LOVE STORY, BUT I'M SURPRISED IT'S SO DEPRESSING.

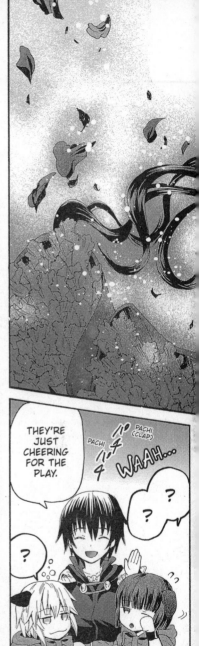

THE UNDEAD HERO TOOK HIS REVENGE ON THE MARQUIS'S FAMILY.

TOSSED OVER THE SIDE OF THE CLIFF, THE PROTAGONIST'S CORPSE WAS BROUGHT BACK TO LIFE.

THEY'RE JUST CHEERING FOR THE PLAY.

PACHI (CLAP)

PACHI

WAAH...

?

?

?

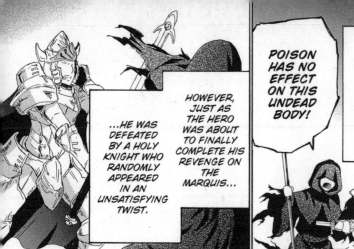

...HE WAS DEFEATED BY A HOLY KNIGHT WHO RANDOMLY APPEARED IN AN UNSATISFYING TWIST.

HOWEVER, JUST AS THE HERO WAS ABOUT TO FINALLY COMPLETE HIS REVENGE ON THE MARQUIS...

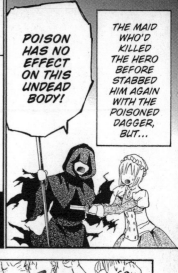

POISON HAS NO EFFECT ON THIS UNDEAD BODY!

THE MAID WHO'D KILLED THE HERO BEFORE STABBED HIM AGAIN WITH THE POISONED DAGGER, BUT...

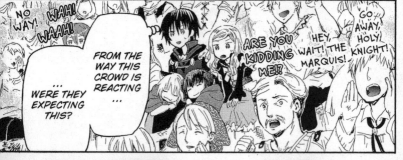

NO WAY! WAH! WAAH!

...WERE THEY EXPECTING THIS?

FROM THE WAY THIS CROWD IS REACTING...

ARE YOU KIDDING ME!?

HEY, WAIT! THE MARQUIS!

GO AWAY, HOLY KNIGHT!

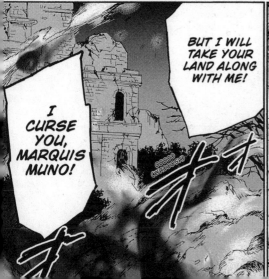

I CURSE YOU, MARQUIS MUNO!

BUT I WILL TAKE YOUR LAND ALONG WITH ME!

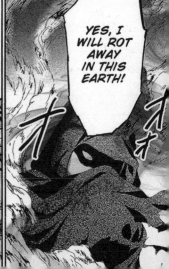

YES, I WILL ROT AWAY IN THIS EARTH!

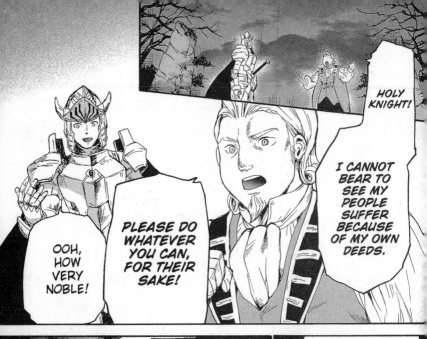

HOLY KNIGHT!

I CANNOT BEAR TO SEE MY PEOPLE SUFFER BECAUSE OF MY OWN DEEDS.

PLEASE DO WHATEVER YOU CAN, FOR THEIR SAKE!

OOH, HOW VERY NOBLE!

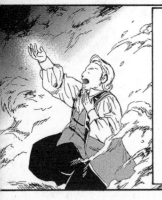

IN THE END, THE MARQUIS SACRIFICED HIMSELF TO PROTECT HIS PEOPLE, AND THE PLAY CONCLUDED WITH THE SCENE OF HIM TAKING THE CURSE FROM HIS LAND AT THE COST OF HIS OWN LIFE.

JUST AS ONE WOULD EXPECT FROM THE HEAD OF THE MUNO FAMILY, WHICH HAS EXISTED SINCE THE ERA OF THE ANCESTRAL KING YAMATO!

...I FEEL LIKE THE MARQUIS'S PERSONALITY CHANGED ALL OF A SUDDEN.

THE HOLY KNIGHT SURE IS PRAISING HIM A LOT.

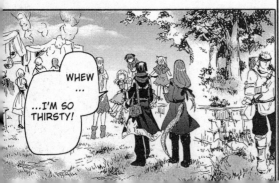

WHEW...

...I'M SO THIRSTY!

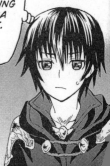

THANK YOU, SIR!

HERE.

I'M GETTING A BIT HUNGRY TOO.

I'LL GO BUY SOMETHING FROM A FOOD CART.

I BOUGHT SOME FRUIT WATER.

GOKU (GLUG)

GOKU

THANK YOU!

WOULD YOU LIKE SOME TOO, ZENA-SAN?

THANK YOU VERY MUCH.

AND THIS PLACE HAS SOMETHING CALLED "CRAPPES"...

"GABO FRUIT" WAS THAT FANTASY CROP, RIGHT?

GABO FLAT-BREAD?

OH...

WHAT'S THIS...?

I SMELL SOY SAUCE...

NORMAL

THIN, SAVORY, MISO-FLAVORED PANCAKE

FILLED WITH ONIONS

COOKED IN DILUTED SOY SAUCE

THERE WERE NO PREMADE FLATBREADS LEFT, SO I HAD TO WAIT A BIT FOR MY ORDER.

JUUU (SIZZLE)

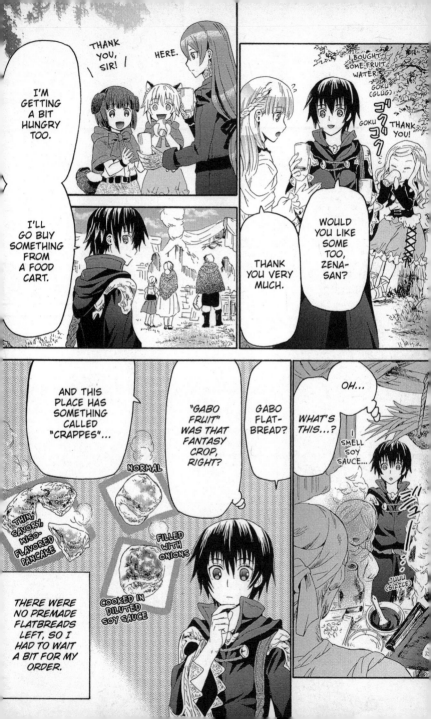

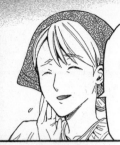

I'M SURE YOU FOUND THE LAST BIT RATHER AWFUL, DIDN'T YOU?

HOW DID YOU ENJOY THE PLAY?

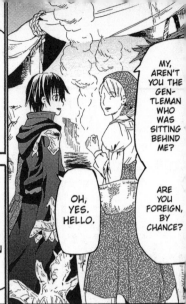

MY, AREN'T YOU THE GENTLEMAN WHO WAS SITTING BEHIND ME?

ARE YOU FOREIGN, BY CHANCE?

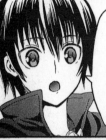

...AND THE MARQUIS'S CHARACTER SUDDENLY CHANGED?

YOU MEAN WHEN THE HOLY KNIGHT SHOWED UP WITHOUT AN INTRODUCTION...

OH, YES. HELLO.

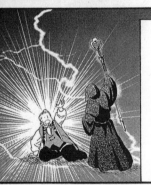

...IT ENDED WITH THE SORCERER TAKING HIS REVENGE ON THE MARQUIS AND THEN BEING DEFEATED BY THE HOLY KNIGHT.

THE WOMAN SAID THAT SOME TWENTY YEARS AGO, WHEN THE PLAY WAS FIRST WRITTEN...

YES, WELL, YOU SEE...

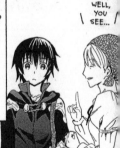

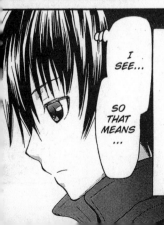

I SEE...

SO THAT MEANS...

...AND IN THE ORIGINAL STORY, THE EVENTS HAD BEEN SET IN MOTION WHEN THE AMOROUS MARQUIS ABDUCTED HER AWAY FROM HER HUSBAND.

FURTHERMORE, PRINCESS LILTIENA HAD BEEN THE DAUGHTER OF A COMMONER...

HOWEVER, IT HAD APPARENTLY BEEN CHANGED DUE TO COMPLAINTS FROM THE NOBILITY.

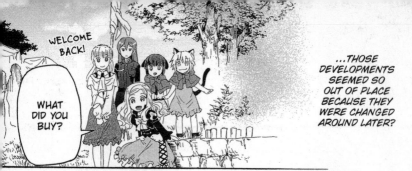

WELCOME BACK!

WHAT DID YOU BUY?

...THOSE DEVELOPMENTS SEEMED SO OUT OF PLACE BECAUSE THEY WERE CHANGED AROUND LATER?

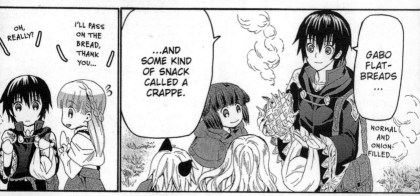

OH, REALLY?

I'LL PASS ON THE BREAD, THANK YOU...

...AND SOME KIND OF SNACK CALLED A CRAPPE.

GABO FLAT-BREADS...

NORMAL AND ONION-FILLED...

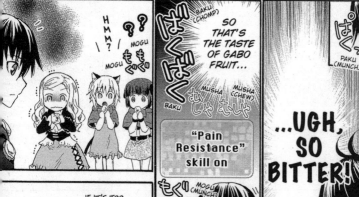

HMM?

MOGU MOGU ぐぐぐ

BAKU (CHOMP)

SO THAT'S THE TASTE OF GABO FRUIT...

ばくばく

MUSHA (CHEW) MUSHA むしゃむしゃ

BAKU

"Pain Resistance" skill on

もぐもぐ

MOGU (MUNCH) MOGU

GOKKUN (GULP) ごっくん。

ばく

PAKU (CMUNCH)

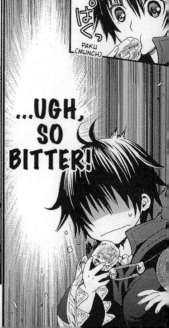

...UGH, SO BITTER!

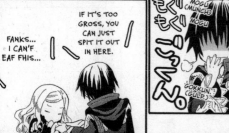

FANKS... I CAN'F EAF FHIS...

IF IT'S TOO GROSS, YOU CAN JUST SPIT IT OUT IN HERE.

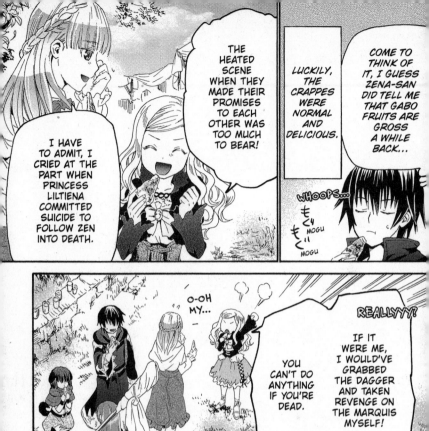

COME TO THINK OF IT, I GUESS ZENA-SAN DID TELL ME THAT GABO FRUITS ARE GROSS A WHILE BACK...

LUCKILY, THE CRAPPES WERE NORMAL AND DELICIOUS.

THE HEATED SCENE WHEN THEY MADE THEIR PROMISES TO EACH OTHER WAS TOO MUCH TO BEAR!

I HAVE TO ADMIT, I CRIED AT THE PART WHEN PRINCESS LILTIENA COMMITTED SUICIDE TO FOLLOW ZEN INTO DEATH.

WHOOPS...

MOGU MOGU

O-OH MY...

REALLYYY?

YOU CAN'T DO ANYTHING IF YOU'RE DEAD.

IF IT WERE ME, I WOULD'VE GRABBED THE DAGGER AND TAKEN REVENGE ON THE MARQUIS MYSELF!

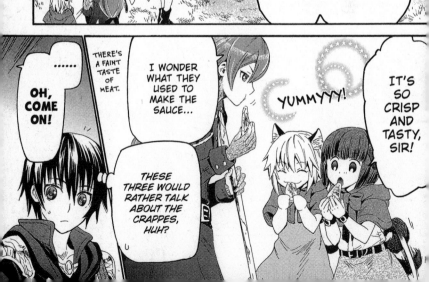

OH, COME ON!

THERE'S A FAINT TASTE OF MEAT.

I WONDER WHAT THEY USED TO MAKE THE SAUCE...

THESE THREE WOULD RATHER TALK ABOUT THE CRAPPES, HUH?

YUMMYYY!

IT'S SO CRISP AND TASTY, SIR!

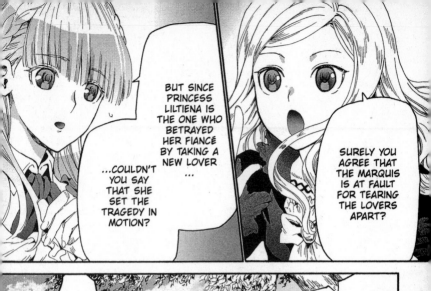

BUT SINCE PRINCESS LILTIENA IS THE ONE WHO BETRAYED HER FIANCÉ BY TAKING A NEW LOVER...

...COULDN'T YOU SAY THAT SHE SET THE TRAGEDY IN MOTION?

SURELY YOU AGREE THAT THE MARQUIS IS AT FAULT FOR TEARING THE LOVERS APART?

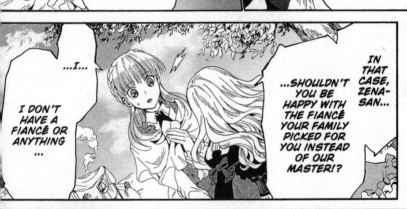

...I...

I DON'T HAVE A FIANCÉ OR ANYTHING...

...SHOULDN'T YOU BE HAPPY WITH THE FIANCÉ YOUR FAMILY PICKED FOR YOU INSTEAD OF OUR MASTER!?

IN THAT CASE, ZENA-SAN...

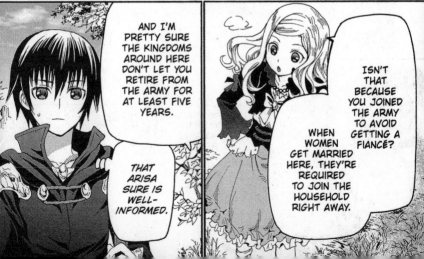

AND I'M PRETTY SURE THE KINGDOMS AROUND HERE DON'T LET YOU RETIRE FROM THE ARMY FOR AT LEAST FIVE YEARS.

THAT ARISA SURE IS WELL-INFORMED.

ISN'T THAT BECAUSE YOU JOINED THE ARMY TO AVOID GETTING A FIANCÉ?

WHEN WOMEN GET MARRIED HERE, THEY'RE REQUIRED TO JOIN THE HOUSEHOLD RIGHT AWAY.

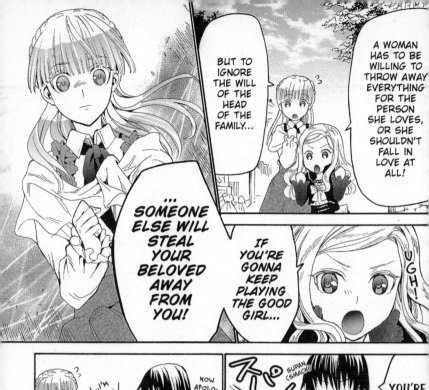

A WOMAN HAS TO BE WILLING TO THROW AWAY EVERYTHING FOR THE PERSON SHE LOVES, OR SHE SHOULDN'T FALL IN LOVE AT ALL!

BUT TO IGNORE THE WILL OF THE HEAD OF THE FAMILY...

...SOMEONE ELSE WILL STEAL YOUR BELOVED AWAY FROM YOU!

IF YOU'RE GONNA KEEP PLAYING THE GOOD GIRL...

UGH!

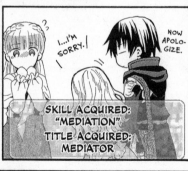

?? I...I'M SORRY.

NOW APOLO-GIZE.

SKILL ACQUIRED:
"MEDIATION"
TITLE ACQUIRED:
MEDIATOR

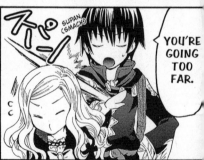

スパーン SUPAN (SMACK)

YOU'RE GOING TOO FAR.

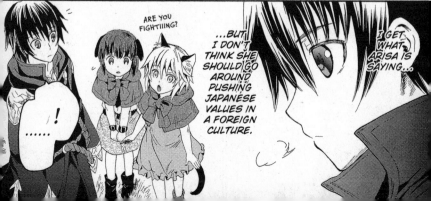

ARE YOU FIGHTIIING?

...BUT I DON'T THINK SHE SHOULD GO AROUND PUSHING JAPANESE VALUES IN A FOREIGN CULTURE.

I GET WHAT ARISA IS SAYING...

.......!

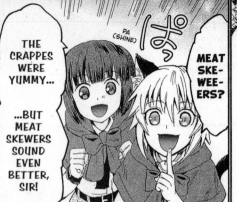

THE CRAPPES WERE YUMMY...

...BUT MEAT SKEWERS SOUND EVEN BETTER, SIR!

PA (SHINE)

MEAT SKE-WEE-ERS?

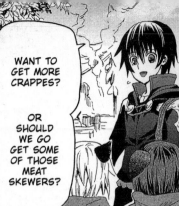

WANT TO GET MORE CRAPPES?

OR SHOULD WE GO GET SOME OF THOSE MEAT SKEWERS?

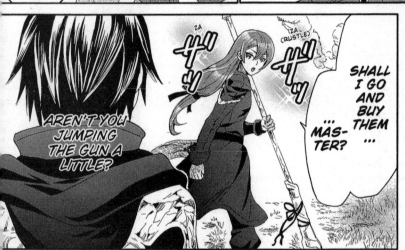

ZA (RUSTLE)

AREN'T YOU JUMPING THE GUN A LITTLE?

...MÄS-TER?...

SHALL I GO AND BUY THEM...

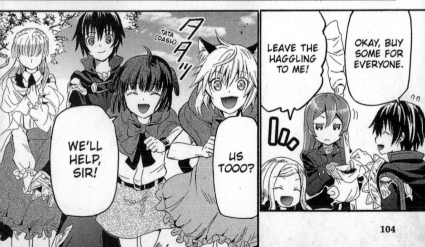

TATA (DASH)

WE'LL HELP, SIR!

US TOOO?

LEAVE THE HAGGLING TO ME!

OKAY, BUY SOME FOR EVERYONE.

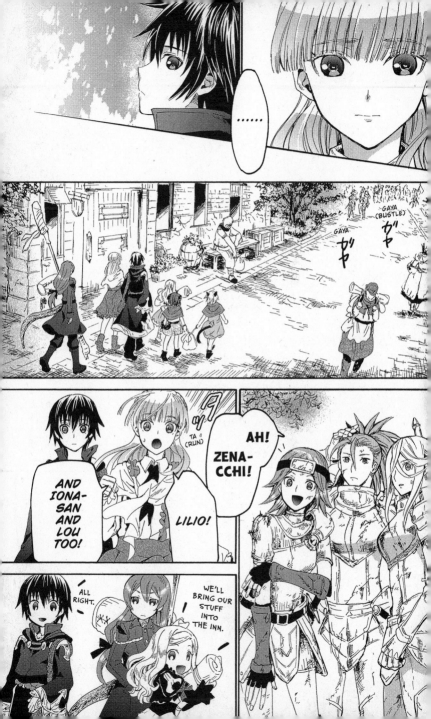

......

GAYA
(BUSTLE)

GAYA

AND IONA-SAN AND LOU TOO!

TA (CRUN)

LILIO!

AH! ZENA-CCHI!

ALL RIGHT.

WE'LL BRING OUR STUFF INTO THE INN.

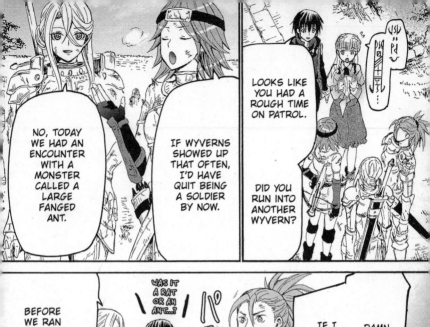

LOOKS LIKE YOU HAD A ROUGH TIME ON PATROL.

DID YOU RUN INTO ANOTHER WYVERN?

NO, TODAY WE HAD AN ENCOUNTER WITH A MONSTER CALLED A LARGE FANGED ANT.

IF WYVERNS SHOWED UP THAT OFTEN, I'D HAVE QUIT BEING A SOLDIER BY NOW.

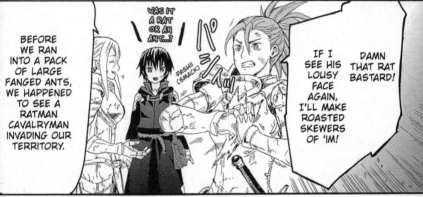

BEFORE WE RAN INTO A PACK OF LARGE FANGED ANTS, WE HAPPENED TO SEE A RATMAN CAVALRYMAN INVADING OUR TERRITORY.

WAS IT A RAT OR AN ANT..?

-PASHI! (SMACK)

DAMN THAT RAT BASTARD!

IF I SEE HIS LOUSY FACE AGAIN, I'LL MAKE ROASTED SKEWERS OF 'IM!

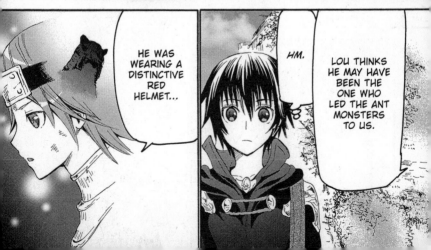

HE WAS WEARING A DISTINCTIVE RED HELMET...

HM.

LOU THINKS HE MAY HAVE BEEN THE ONE WHO LED THE ANT MONSTERS TO US.

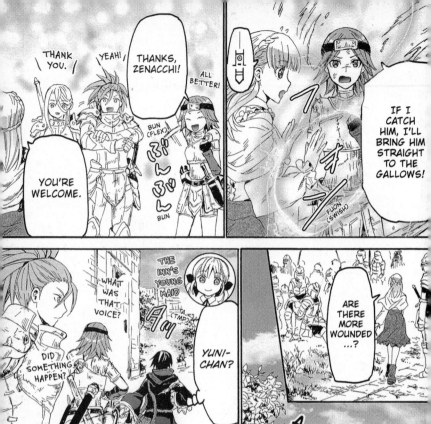

THANK YOU.

YEAH!

THANKS, ZENACCHI!

ALL BETTER!

BUN (FLEX)

ぷんぷん

BUN

YOU'RE WELCOME.

IF I CATCH HIM, I'LL BRING HIM STRAIGHT TO THE GALLOWS!

FUON (SWISH)

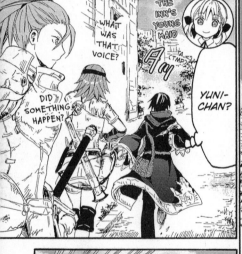

WHAT WAS THAT VOICE?

THE INN'S YOUNG MAID

タッ (TMP)

YUNI-CHAN?

DID SOMETHING HAPPEN?

ARE THERE MORE WOUNDED...?

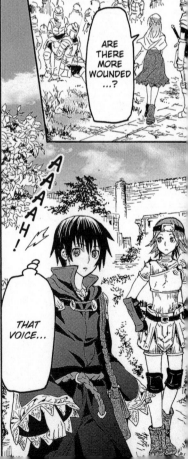

AAAAH!

THAT VOICE...

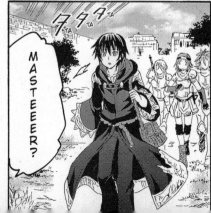

タッタッタッ TA TA TA

MASTEEER?

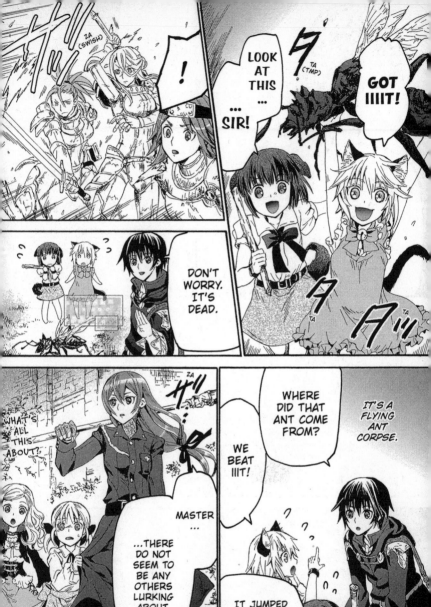

!

LOOK AT THIS ... SIR!

TA (TMP)

GOT IIIIT!

DON'T WORRY. IT'S DEAD.

ZA (SWISH)

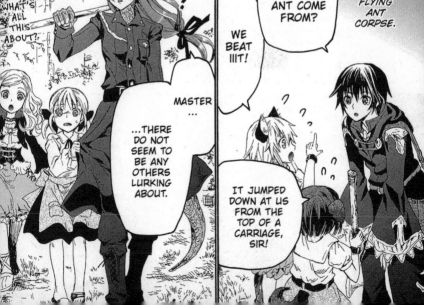

WHAT'S ALL THIS ABOUT?

ZA

WHERE DID THAT ANT COME FROM?

IT'S A FLYING ANT CORPSE.

WE BEAT IIIIT!

MASTER ...

...THERE DO NOT SEEM TO BE ANY OTHERS LURKING ABOUT.

IT JUMPED DOWN AT US FROM THE TOP OF A CARRIAGE, SIR!

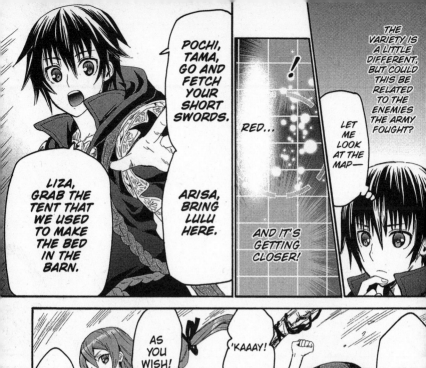

POCHI, TAMA, GO AND FETCH YOUR SHORT SWORDS.

ARISA, BRING LULU HERE.

LIZA, GRAB THE TENT THAT WE USED TO MAKE THE BED IN THE BARN.

RED...

!

AND IT'S GETTING CLOSER!

LET ME LOOK AT THE MAP—

THE VARIETY IS A LITTLE DIFFERENT, BUT COULD THIS BE RELATED TO THE ENEMIES THE ARMY FOUGHT?

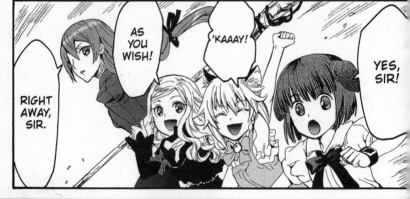

RIGHT AWAY, SIR.

AS YOU WISH!

'KAAAY!

YES, SIR.

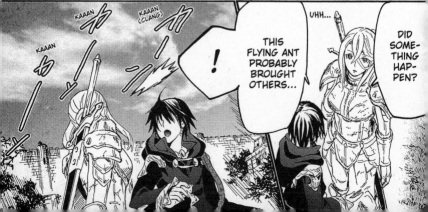

KAAAN

KAAAN

KAAAN (CLANG)

!

THIS FLYING ANT PROBABLY BROUGHT OTHERS...

UHH...

DID SOMETHING HAPPEN?

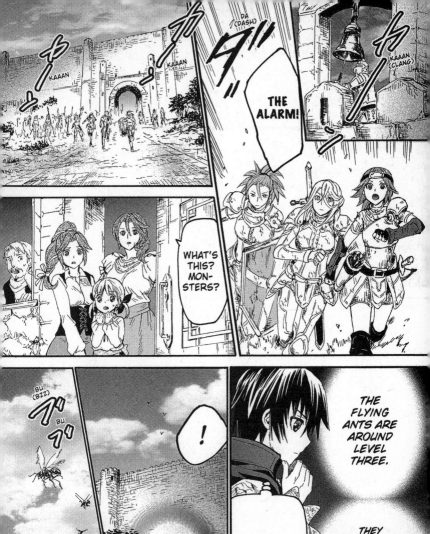
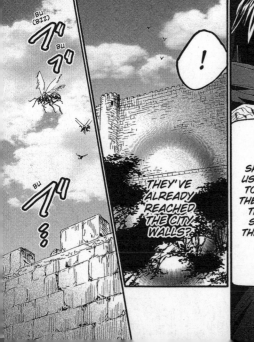

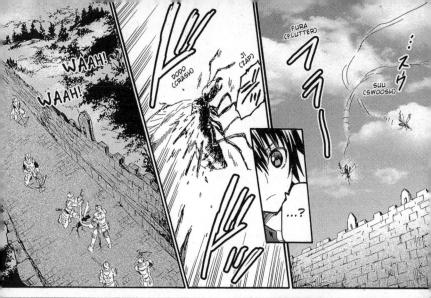

WAAH!

WAAH!

DODO (CRASH)

JI (ZAP)

FURA (FLUTTER)

SUU (SWOOSH)

...?

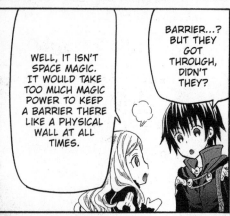

WELL, IT ISN'T SPACE MAGIC. IT WOULD TAKE TOO MUCH MAGIC POWER TO KEEP A BARRIER THERE LIKE A PHYSICAL WALL AT ALL TIMES.

BARRIER...? BUT THEY GOT THROUGH, DIDN'T THEY?

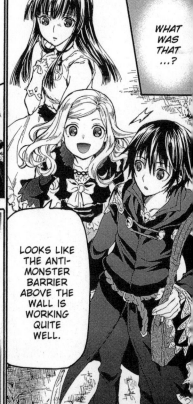

WHAT WAS THAT ...?

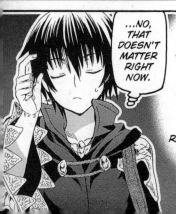

...NO, THAT DOESN'T MATTER RIGHT NOW.

BUT DIDN'T THE BARRIER AT THE VALLEY OF DRAGONS GIVE ME SOME PHYSICAL RESISTANCE?

LOOKS LIKE THE ANTI-MONSTER BARRIER ABOVE THE WALL IS WORKING QUITE WELL.

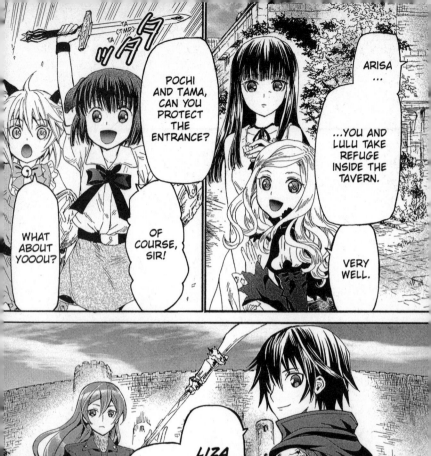

POCHI AND TAMA, CAN YOU PROTECT THE ENTRANCE?

OF COURSE, SIR!

WHAT ABOUT YOOOU?

ARISA...

...YOU AND LULU TAKE REFUGE INSIDE THE TAVERN.

VERY WELL.

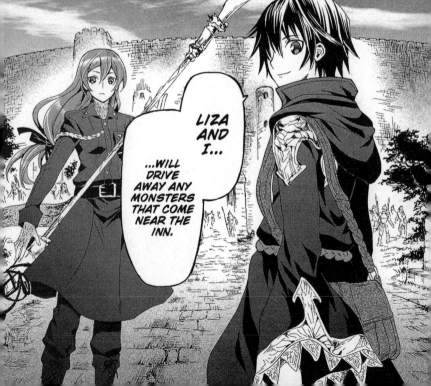

LIZA AND I...

...WILL DRIVE AWAY ANY MONSTERS THAT COME NEAR THE INN.

CHAPTER 18: MARAUDERS AT THE GATE

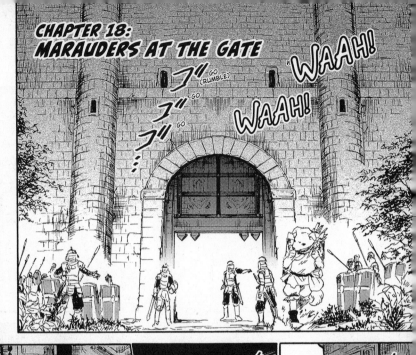

ブ GO
(RUMBLE)

'WAAH!

WAAH!

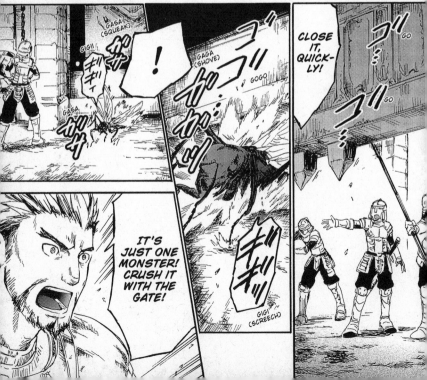

GIGI
キィ

GASA
(SQUEAK)

ガサ

!

GAGA
(SHOVE)

ガガ
GOGO
ブ GO

CLOSE IT, QUICK-LY!

ブ GO

IT'S JUST ONE MONSTER! CRUSH IT WITH THE GATE!

キィ

GIGI
(SCREECH)

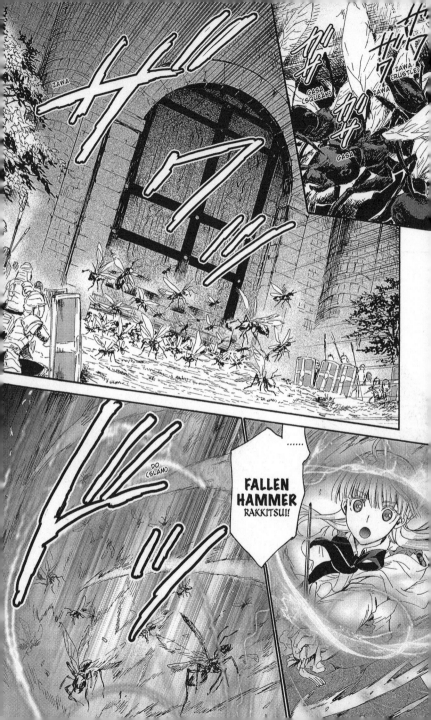

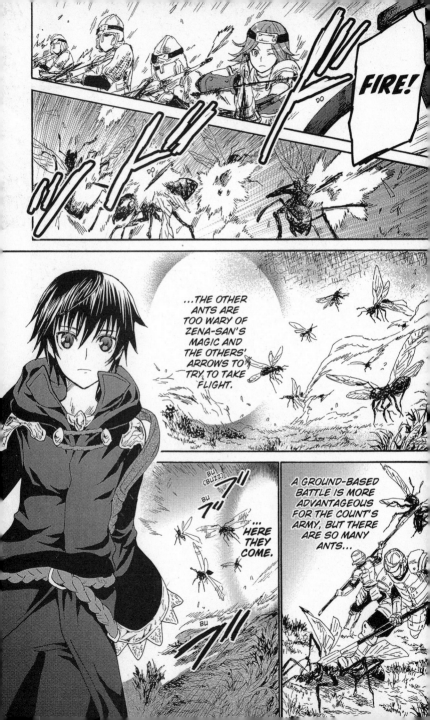

FIRE!

...THE OTHER ANTS ARE TOO WARY OF ZENA-SAN'S MAGIC AND THE OTHERS' ARROWS TO TRY TO TAKE FLIGHT.

BU (BUZZ)
BU

...HERE THEY COME.

BU

A GROUND-BASED BATTLE IS MORE ADVANTAGEOUS FOR THE COUNT'S ARMY, BUT THERE ARE SO MANY ANTS...

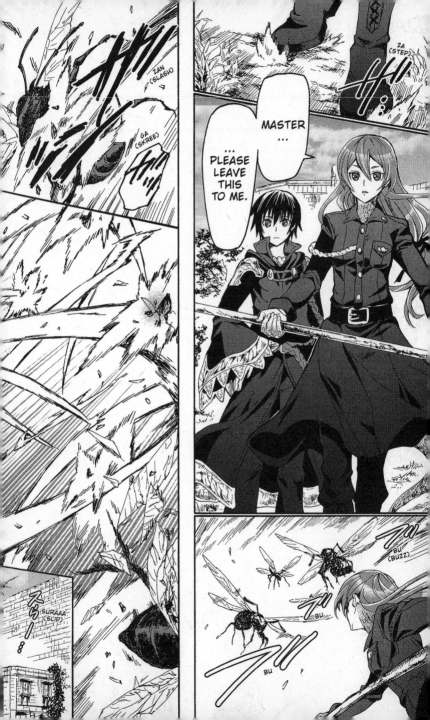

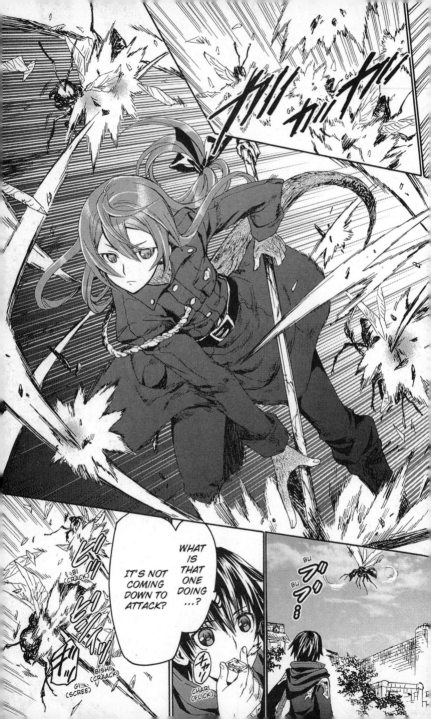

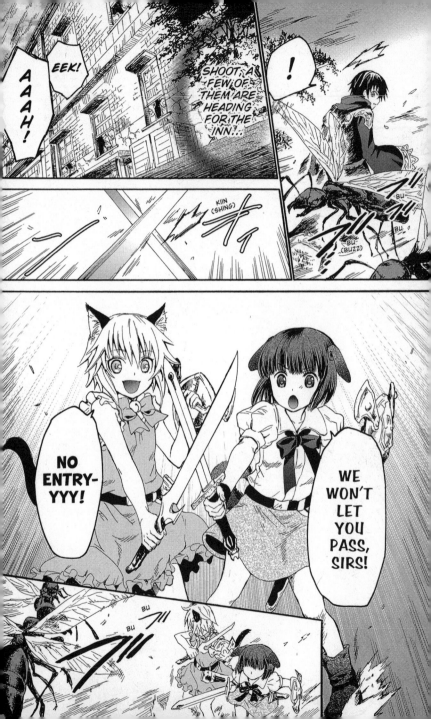

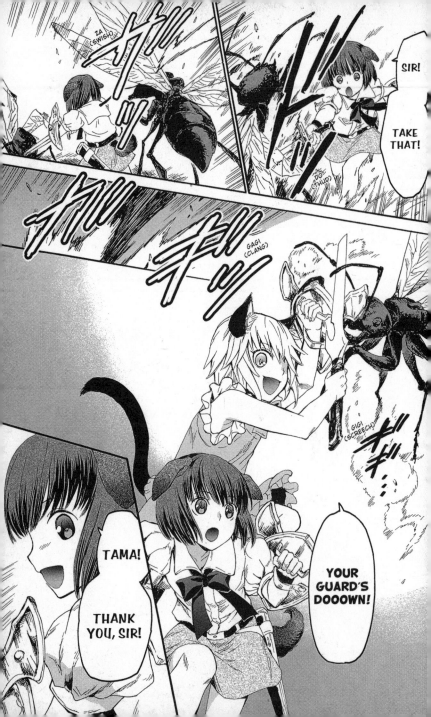

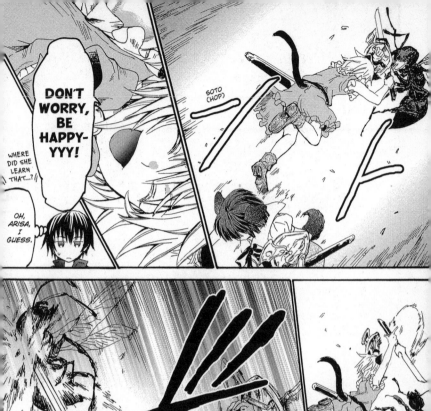

DON'T WORRY, BE HAPPY-YYY!

WHERE DID SHE LEARN THAT...?

OH, ARISA, I GUESS.

SOTO (HOP)

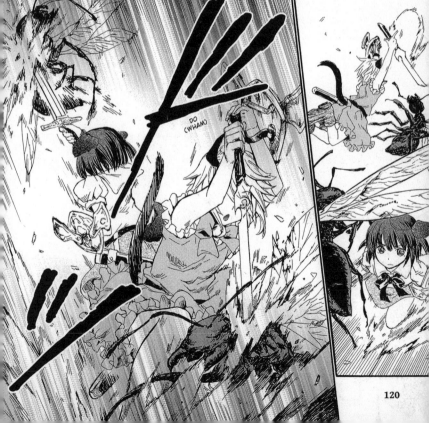

DO (WHAM)

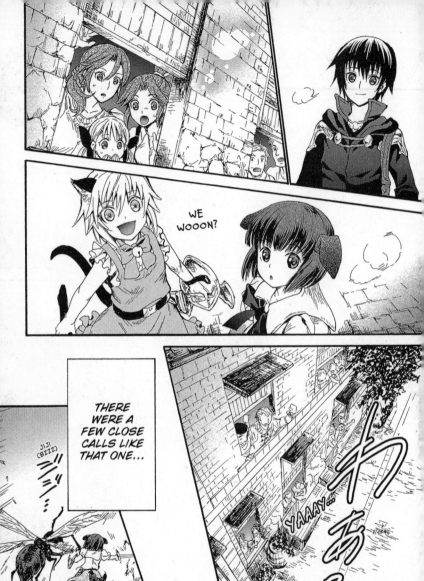

WE
WOOON?

THERE
WERE A
FEW CLOSE
CALLS LIKE
THAT ONE...

JIJ
(BZZZ)

YAAAY...

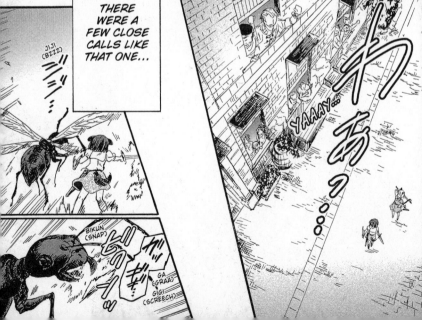

BIKUN
(SNAP)

GA
(GRAA)
GIGI
(SCREECH)

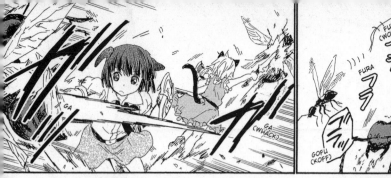

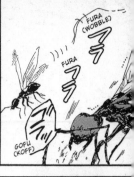

FURA
(WOBBLE)

FURA

GOFU
(KOFF)

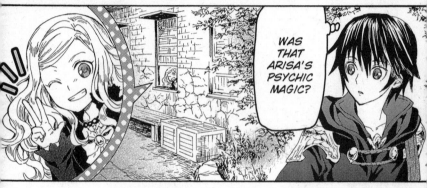

WAS THAT ARISA'S PSYCHIC MAGIC?

NADI-SAN LOOKS TO BE HIDING IN THE BASEMENT, SO SHE SHOULD BE FINE, BUT...

...I'LL GO HELP JUST IN CASE.

......

IT LOOKS LIKE A FEW ANTS ARE CHARGING NADI-SAN'S GENERAL GOODS STORE.

IN LESS THAN A HALF HOUR...

...MOST OF THE ANTS IN THE PLAZA...

WAA!

WAA!

...HAD BEEN TAKEN DOWN...

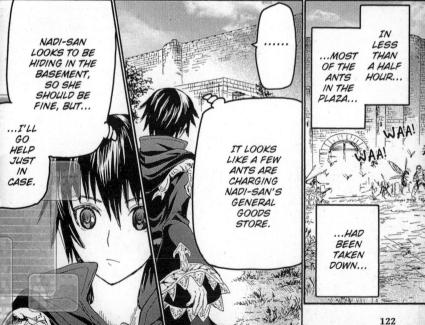

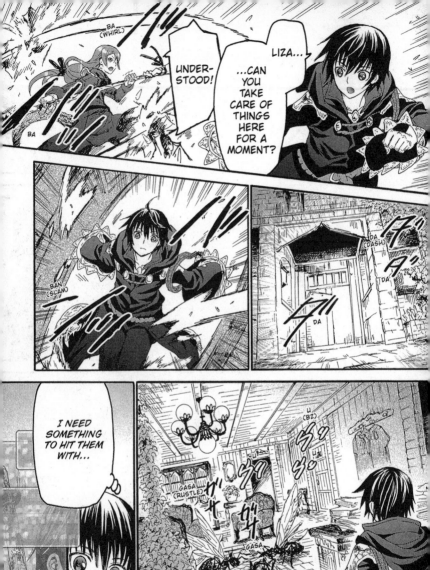

LIZA...

...CAN YOU TAKE CARE OF THINGS HERE FOR A MOMENT?

UNDERSTOOD!

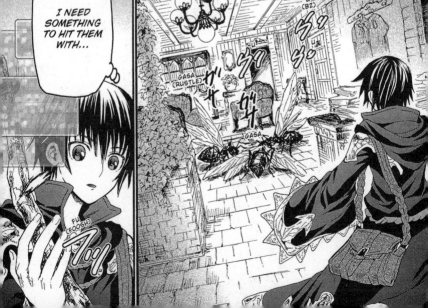

I NEED SOMETHING TO HIT THEM WITH...

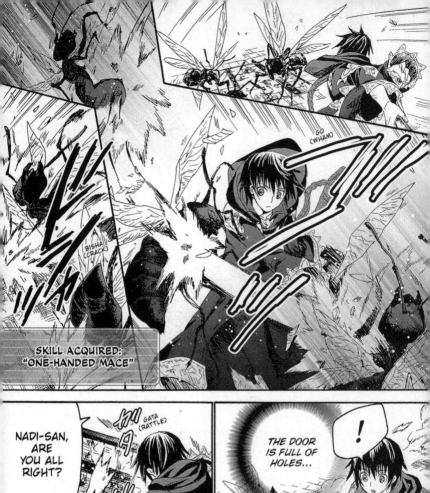

GO
(WHAM)

BISHA
(CRACK)

SKILL ACQUIRED:
"ONE-HANDED MACE"

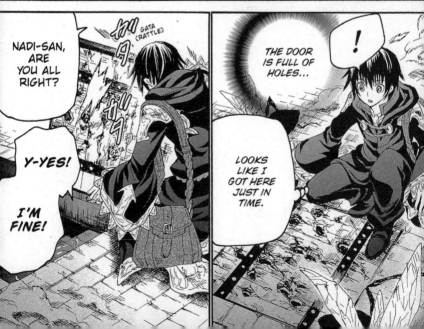

GATA
(RATTLE)

NADI-SAN,
ARE
YOU ALL
RIGHT?

Y-YES!

I'M
FINE!

GATA

!

THE DOOR
IS FULL OF
HOLES...

LOOKS
LIKE I
GOT HERE
JUST IN
TIME.

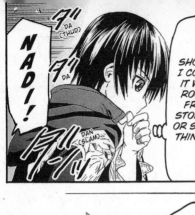

NADI!

DA (THUD)

DA

DAN (SLAM)

SHOULD I COVER IT WITH ROCKS FROM STORAGE OR SOMETHING...?

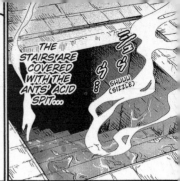

THE STAIRS ARE COVERED WITH THE ANTS' ACID SPIT...

SHULU (SIZZLE)

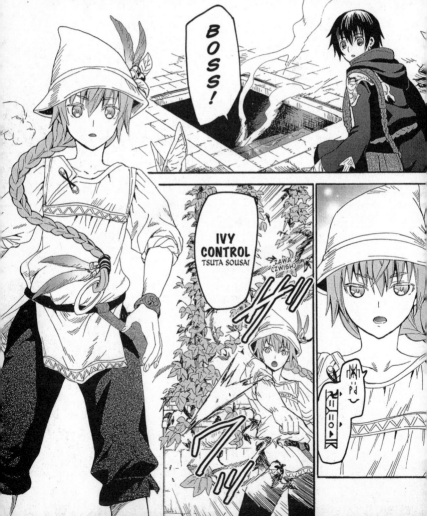

BOSS!

IVY CONTROL
TSUTA SOUSA!

ZAWA (CZWISH)

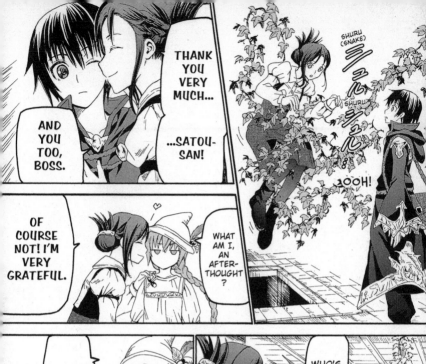

THANK YOU VERY MUCH...

...SATOU-SAN!

AND YOU TOO, BOSS.

SHURU (SNAKE)

OOH!

OF COURSE NOT! I'M VERY GRATEFUL.

WHAT AM I, AN AFTERTHOUGHT?

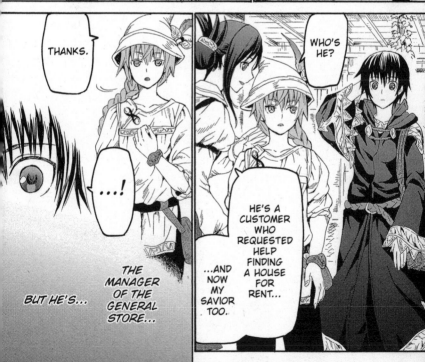

THANKS.

...!

WHO'S HE?

THE MANAGER OF THE GENERAL STORE...

BUT HE'S...

HE'S A CUSTOMER WHO REQUESTED HELP FINDING A HOUSE FOR RENT...

...AND NOW MY SAVIOR TOO.

126

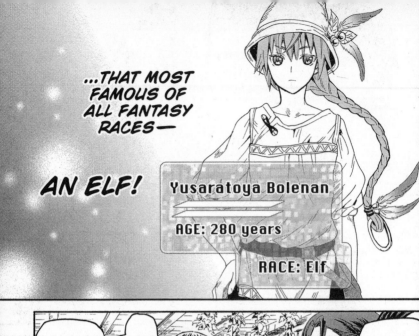

...THAT MOST FAMOUS OF ALL FANTASY RACES—

AN ELF!

Yusaratoya Bolenan

AGE: 280 years

RACE: Elf

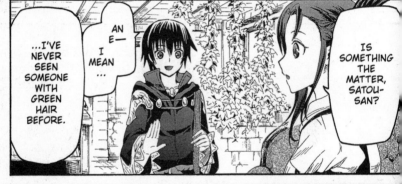

...I'VE NEVER SEEN SOMEONE WITH GREEN HAIR BEFORE.

AN E— I MEAN...

IS SOMETHING THE MATTER, SATOU-SAN?

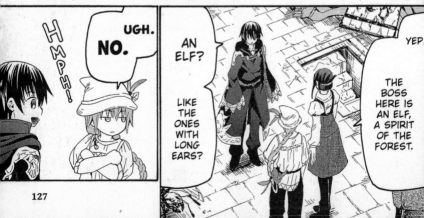

HMPH!

UGH. NO.

AN ELF? LIKE THE ONES WITH LONG EARS?

YEP!

THE BOSS HERE IS AN ELF, A SPIRIT OF THE FOREST.

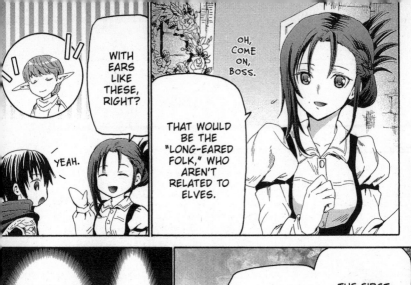

WITH EARS LIKE THESE, RIGHT?

YEAH.

OH, COME ON, BOSS.

THAT WOULD BE THE "LONG-EARED FOLK," WHO AREN'T RELATED TO ELVES.

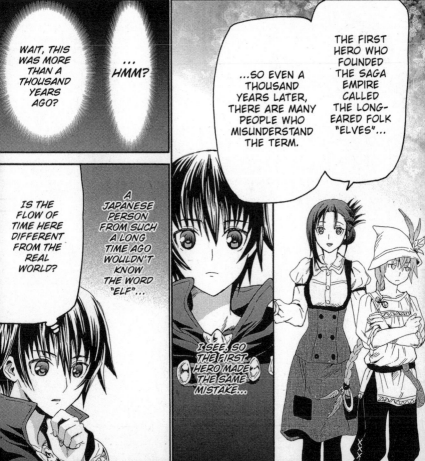

WAIT, THIS WAS MORE THAN A THOUSAND YEARS AGO?

...HMM?

THE FIRST HERO WHO FOUNDED THE SAGA EMPIRE CALLED THE LONG-EARED FOLK "ELVES"...

...SO EVEN A THOUSAND YEARS LATER, THERE ARE MANY PEOPLE WHO MISUNDERSTAND THE TERM.

IS THE FLOW OF TIME HERE DIFFERENT FROM THE REAL WORLD?

A JAPANESE PERSON FROM SUCH A LONG TIME AGO WOULDN'T KNOW THE WORD "ELF"...

I SEE, SO THE FIRST HERO MADE THE SAME MISTAKE...

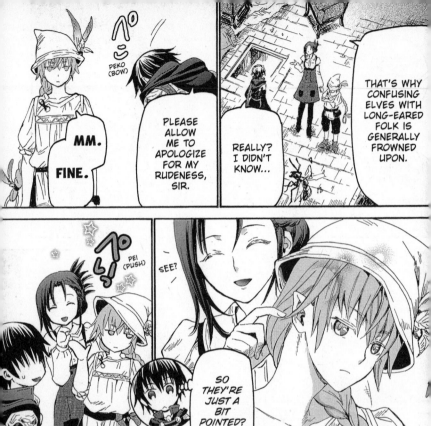

PEKO (BOW)

MM. FINE.

PLEASE ALLOW ME TO APOLOGIZE FOR MY RUDENESS, SIR.

REALLY? I DIDN'T KNOW...

THAT'S WHY CONFUSING ELVES WITH LONG-EARED FOLK IS GENERALLY FROWNED UPON.

PEI (PUSH)

SEE?

SO THEY'RE JUST A BIT POINTED?

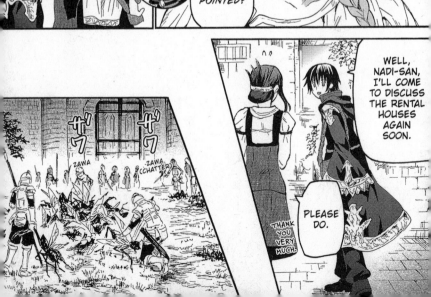

ZAWA

ZAWA (CHATTER)

WELL, NADI-SAN, I'LL COME TO DISCUSS THE RENTAL HOUSES AGAIN SOON.

THANK YOU VERY MUCH.

PLEASE DO.

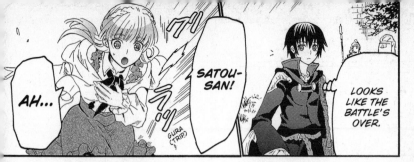

AH...

SATOU-SAN!

LOOKS LIKE THE BATTLE'S OVER.

GURA (TRIP)

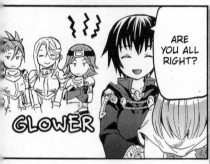

ARE YOU ALL RIGHT?

GLOWER

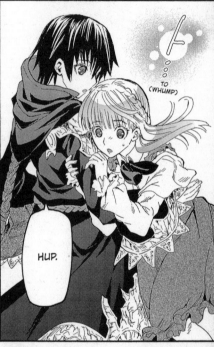

TO (WHUMP)

HUP.

ACCORDING TO ZENA-SAN, THERE HADN'T BEEN ANY CIVILIAN OR MILITARY CASUALTIES.

EVEN THE INJURED ONLY HAD MINOR WOUNDS, AND PRIESTS HAD ALREADY STARTED TREATING THEM.

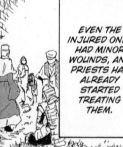

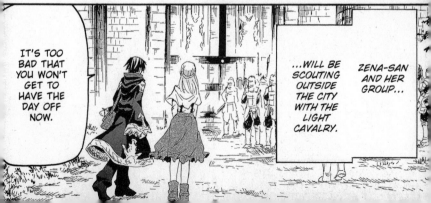

IT'S TOO BAD THAT YOU WON'T GET TO HAVE THE DAY OFF NOW.

ZENA-SAN AND HER GROUP...

...WILL BE SCOUTING OUTSIDE THE CITY WITH THE LIGHT CAVALRY.

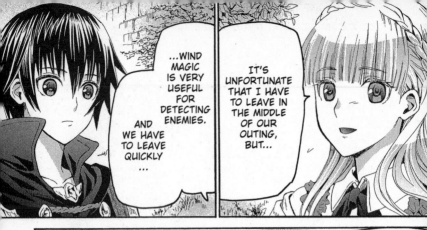

...WIND MAGIC IS VERY USEFUL FOR DETECTING ENEMIES.

AND WE HAVE TO LEAVE QUICKLY...

IT'S UNFORTUNATE THAT I HAVE TO LEAVE IN THE MIDDLE OF OUR OUTING, BUT...

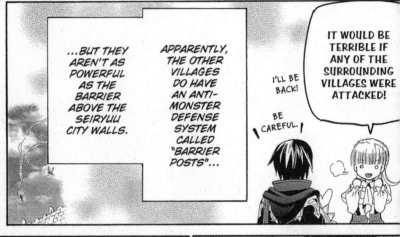

...BUT THEY AREN'T AS POWERFUL AS THE BARRIER ABOVE THE SEIRYUU CITY WALLS.

APPARENTLY, THE OTHER VILLAGES DO HAVE AN ANTI-MONSTER DEFENSE SYSTEM CALLED "BARRIER POSTS"...

I'LL BE BACK!

BE CAREFUL.

IT WOULD BE TERRIBLE IF ANY OF THE SURROUNDING VILLAGES WERE ATTACKED!

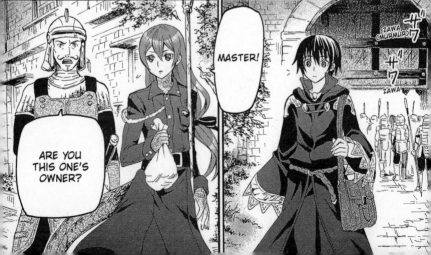

MASTER!

ARE YOU THIS ONE'S OWNER?

ZAWA (MURMUR)

ZAWA

FLYING ANT CORES, HUH?

YES. MY NAME IS SATOU.

GASA (RUSTLE)

MONSTER CORES MUST BE SOLD TO THE LOCAL GOVERNMENT IMMEDIATELY.

HAND THEM OVER, PLEASE.

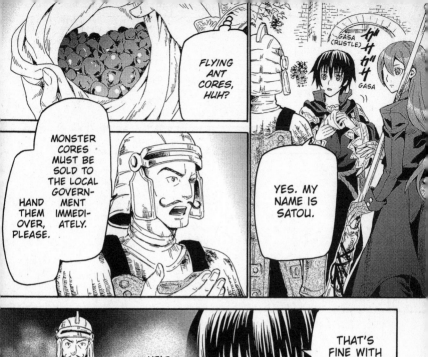

...HE'S FROM THE ACCOUNTING DEPARTMENT OF THE COUNT'S ARMY.

THAT'S FINE WITH ME, BUT SHOULDN'T TENDING TO THE INJURED AND CLEANUP COME FIRST?

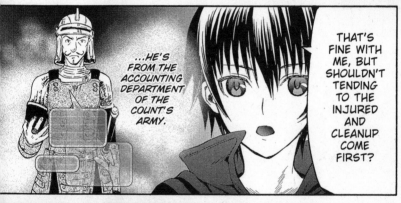

THAT'S SOMEONE ELSE'S JOB.

WAIT JUST A MOMENT, PLEASE.

LIZA AND THE GIRLS' HARD-EARNED CORES...

ZA (THUD)

BA (GRAB)

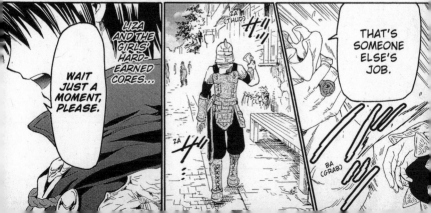

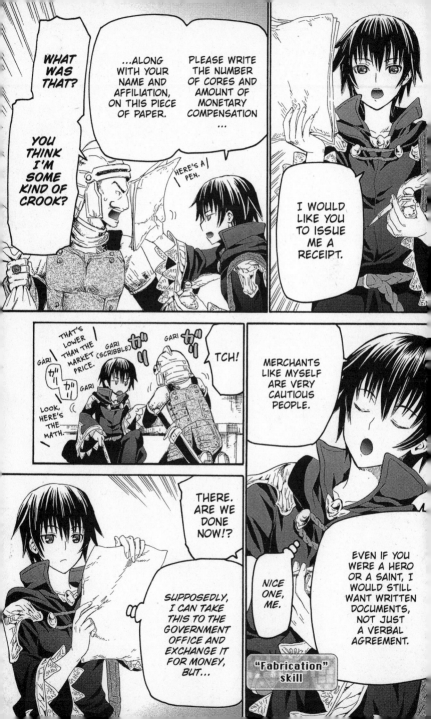

WHAT WAS THAT?

YOU THINK I'M SOME KIND OF CROOK?

...ALONG WITH YOUR NAME AND AFFILIATION, ON THIS PIECE OF PAPER.

HERE'S A PEN.

PLEASE WRITE THE NUMBER OF CORES AND AMOUNT OF MONETARY COMPENSATION...

I WOULD LIKE YOU TO ISSUE ME A RECEIPT.

GARI
GARI (SCRIBBLE)
GARI

THAT'S LOWER THAN THE MARKET PRICE.

LOOK, HERE'S THE MATH.

TCH!

MERCHANTS LIKE MYSELF ARE VERY CAUTIOUS PEOPLE.

THERE. ARE WE DONE NOW!?

SUPPOSEDLY, I CAN TAKE THIS TO THE GOVERNMENT OFFICE AND EXCHANGE IT FOR MONEY, BUT...

NICE ONE, ME.

EVEN IF YOU WERE A HERO OR A SAINT, I WOULD STILL WANT WRITTEN DOCUMENTS, NOT JUST A VERBAL AGREEMENT.

"Fabrication" skill

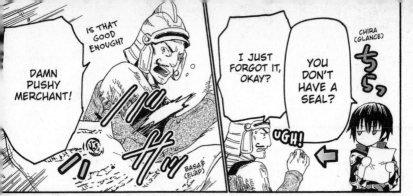

IS THAT GOOD ENOUGH?

DAMN PUSHY MERCHANT!

I JUST FORGOT IT, OKAY?

YOU DON'T HAVE A SEAL?

CHIRA (GLANCE)

ち...っ

BASA (FLAP)

UGH!

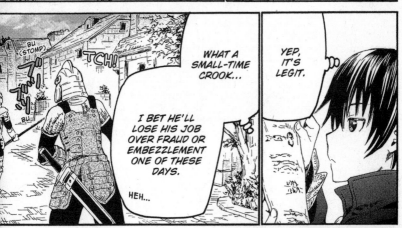

BU (STOMP)

TCH!

BU

WHAT A SMALL-TIME CROOK...

I BET HE'LL LOSE HIS JOB OVER FRAUD OR EMBEZZLEMENT ONE OF THESE DAYS.

HEH...

YEP, IT'S LEGIT.

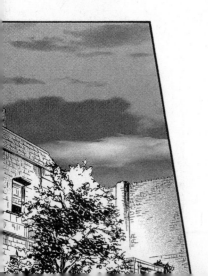

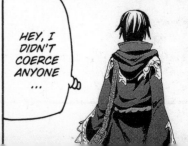

SKILLS ACQUIRED:
"CALCULATION"
"COERCION"

TITLES ACQUIRED:
BEGINNER MERCHANT
GRAY MERCHANT

HEY, I DIDN'T COERCE ANYONE...

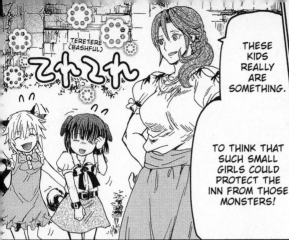

TERETERE
(BASHFUL)

THESE KIDS REALLY ARE SOMETHING.

TO THINK THAT SUCH SMALL GIRLS COULD PROTECT THE INN FROM THOSE MONSTERS!

...HAD SLIPPED IN WITH A CART THAT HAD ARRIVED AT THE GATEFRONT INN NOT LONG BEFORE.

IT SEEMS THE FLYING ANT THAT ATTACKED POCHI AND TAMA...

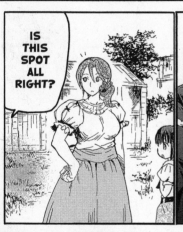

IS THIS SPOT ALL RIGHT?

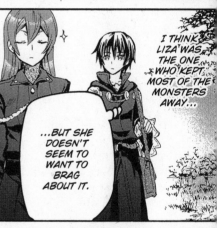

I THINK LIZA WAS THE ONE WHO KEPT MOST OF THE MONSTERS AWAY...

...BUT SHE DOESN'T SEEM TO WANT TO BRAG ABOUT IT.

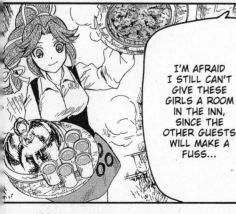

I'M AFRAID I STILL CAN'T GIVE THESE GIRLS A ROOM IN THE INN, SINCE THE OTHER GUESTS WILL MAKE A FUSS...

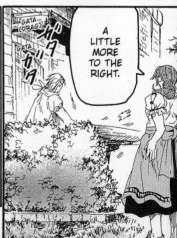

GATA
(DRAG)

GATA

A LITTLE MORE TO THE RIGHT.

AT THE VERY LEAST, LET US TREAT YOU TO SOME OF MY HUSBAND'S MASTERFUL COOKING.

...BUT WE'VE GOT TO THANK THEM SOMEHOW!

JUST WAIT A LITTLE LONGER.

THE SMELL OF HAPPINESS, SIR!

I'M HUNGRYYY!

IT SMELLS GREAT.

...THE SHOCK FROM THE FLYING ANT RAID MADE HER ANEMIC.

ON TOP OF HER ALREADY POOR CONDITION...

THESE FRUITS ARE FOR LULU.

THANKS, YUNI-CHAN.

I GOT WHAT YOU ASKED FOR, SATOU-SAN!

BATA (PITTER)

BATA

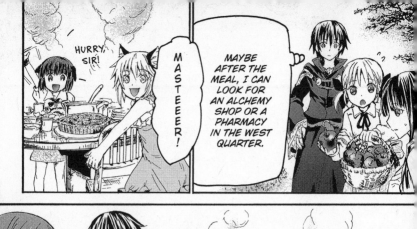

HURRY, SIR!

MASTEEER!

MAYBE AFTER THE MEAL, I CAN LOOK FOR AN ALCHEMY SHOP OR A PHARMACY IN THE WEST QUARTER.

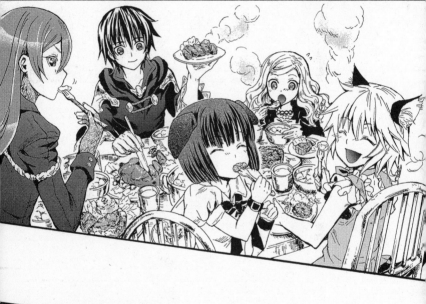

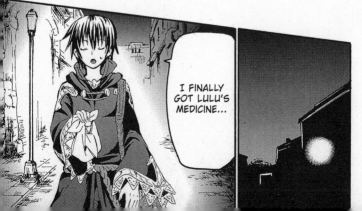

I FINALLY GOT LULU'S MEDICINE...

I PUT ARISA AND LULU TO BED AND CAME TO LOOK FOR A PHARMACY, BUT...

...I RAN INTO A COUPLE OF MERCHANTS I SAVED IN THE LABYRINTH, AND THEY TREATED ME TO A STIFF DRINK. THEN, I ENDED UP TAGGING ALONG WITH THEM TO THEIR FAVORITE BROTHEL...

WELL, IT WAS FUN AND ALL, BUT STILL...

WHEN I FINALLY GOT TO A PHARMACY, THEY TRIED TO CHARGE ME TEN TIMES THE MARKET PRICE.

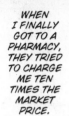

10x

DRIIINK!

AND WHEN I HAGGLED WITH HIM, HE TRIED GIVING ME WEAK STUFF THAT WAS PAST ITS EXPIRATION DATE. I HAD TO POINT IT OUT AND GET HIM TO SWAP IT.

SKILL ACQUIRED: "ANALYZE"

IT WAS THE MENU'S A.R. DISPLAY THAT DID ALL THE ANALYZING, NOT ME...

TCH.

I GUESS I'LL ACTIVATE IT ANYWAY.

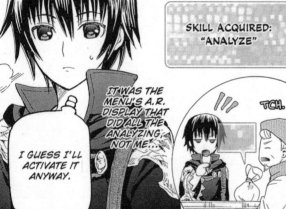

...HM?

HIRA (FLUTTER)

BASA (RUSTLE)

BASA

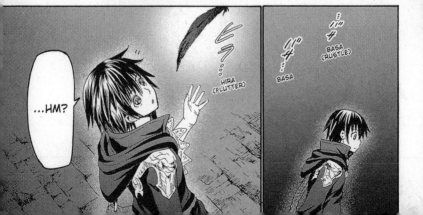

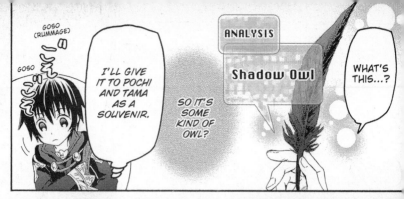

GOSO
(RUMMAGE)

GOSO

I'LL GIVE IT TO POCHI AND TAMA AS A SOUVENIR.

SO IT'S SOME KIND OF OWL?

ANALYSIS

Shadow Owl

WHAT'S THIS...?

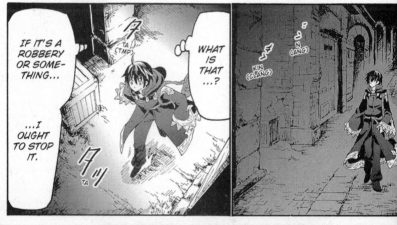

IF IT'S A ROBBERY OR SOMETHING...

...I OUGHT TO STOP IT.

TA
(TMP)

タ

WHAT IS THAT...?

タッ
TA

イ
N (CLANG)

キン
KIN (CLANG)

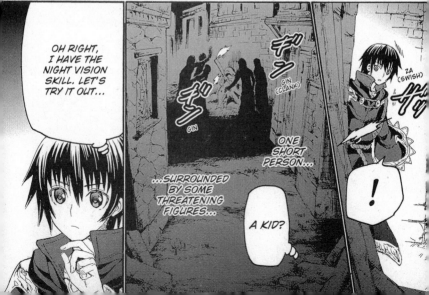

OH RIGHT, I HAVE THE NIGHT VISION SKILL. LET'S TRY IT OUT...

ギン
GIN

ギン
GIN (CLANG)

...SURROUNDED BY SOME THREATENING FIGURES...

ONE SHORT PERSON...

A KID?

ザ
(SWISH)

!

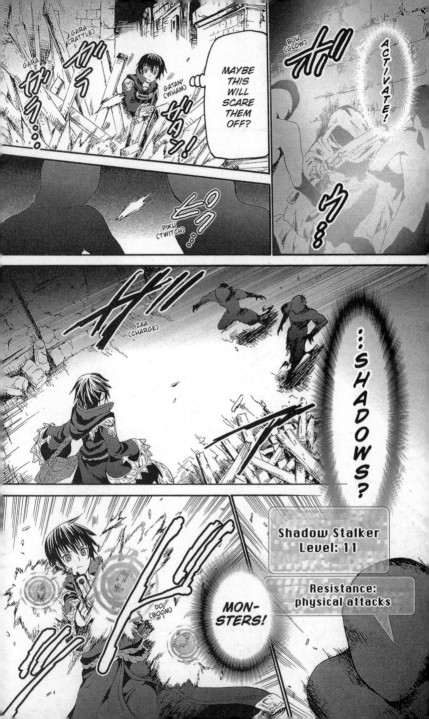

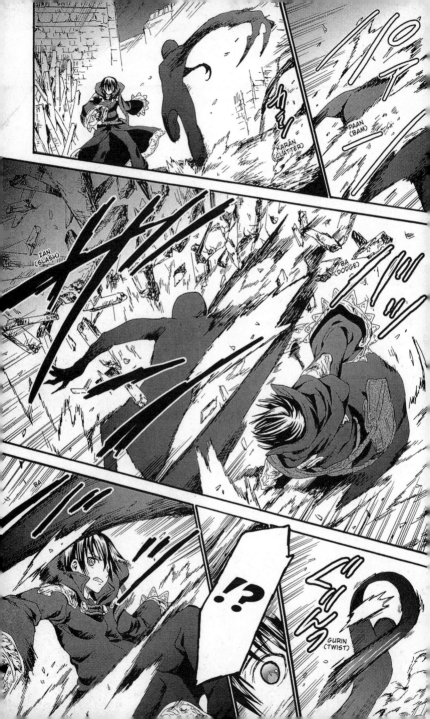

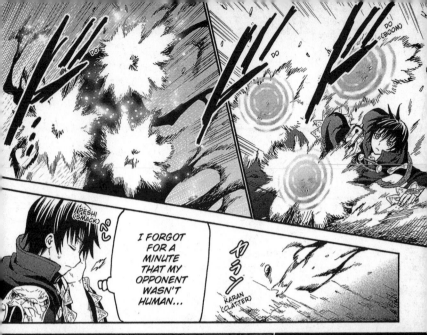

DO
DO
DO (BOOM)

(PESHI (SMACK))

I FORGOT FOR A MINUTE THAT MY OPPONENT WASN'T HUMAN...

カラン
(KARAN (CLATTER))

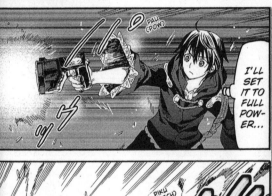

PAU (POW)

I'LL SET IT TO FULL POWER...

...THIS KID IS GOING TO BE KILLED BY THE SHADOWS.

IF I DON'T HURRY UP AND HELP HIM...

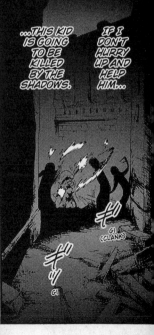

GI (CLANK)

GI

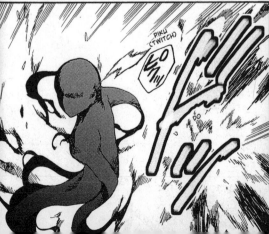

PIKU (TWITCH)

142

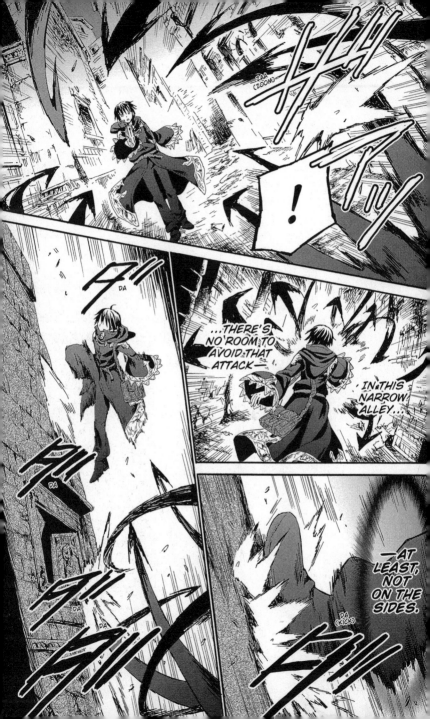

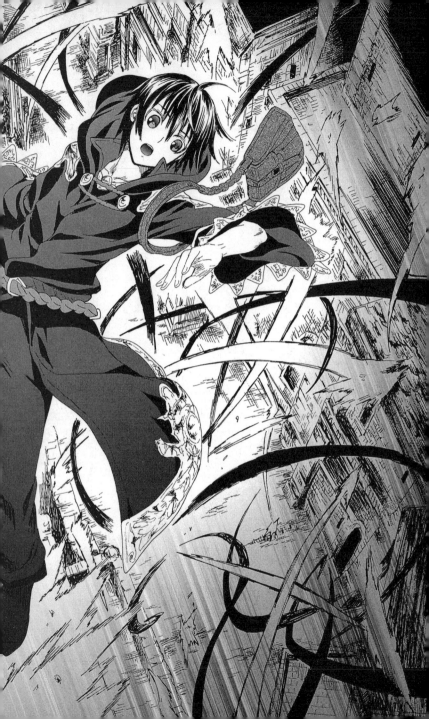

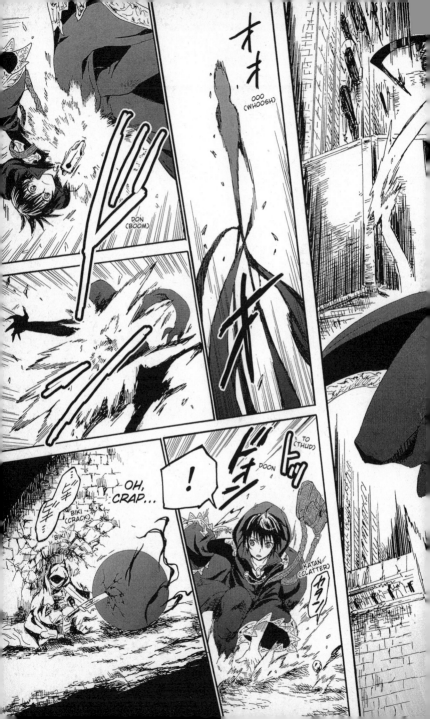

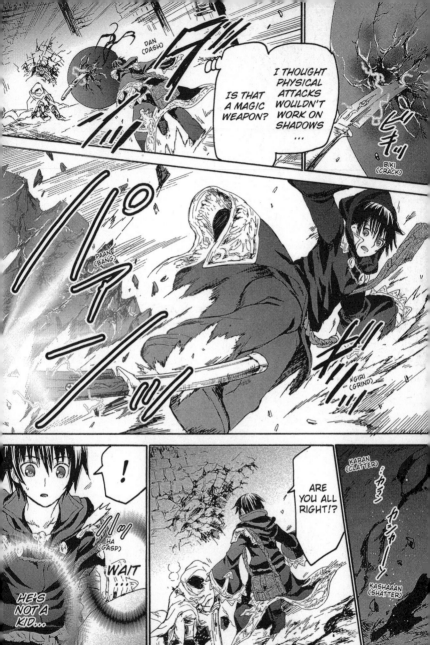

DAN
(DASH)

IS THAT A MAGIC WEAPON?

I THOUGHT PHYSICAL ATTACKS WOULDN'T WORK ON SHADOWS...

BIKI
(CRACK)

PAAN!
(BANG)

NGIRI
(GRIND)

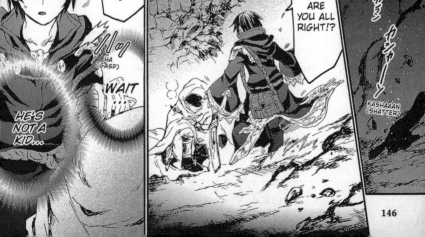

!

HA
(GASP)

WAIT

HE'S NOT A KID...

ARE YOU ALL RIGHT!?

KARAN
(CLATTER)

KASHAAAN
(SHATTER)

146

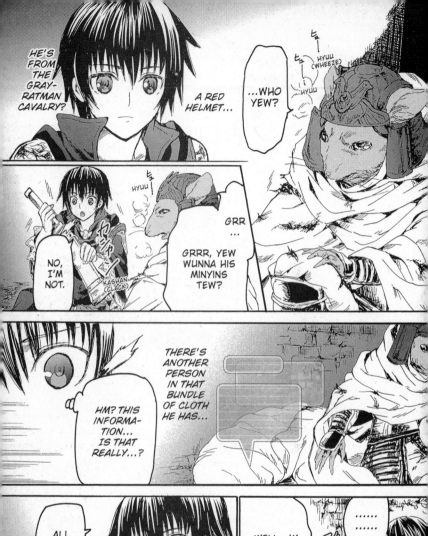

HE'S FROM THE GRAY-RATMAN CAVALRY?

A RED HELMET...

...WHO YEW?

HYUU (WHEEZE)

NO, I'M NOT.

HYUU

KASHAN (CCLACK)

GRR...

GRRR, YEW WUNNA HIS MINYINS TEW?

HM? THIS INFORMATION... IS THAT REALLY...?

THERE'S ANOTHER PERSON IN THAT BUNDLE OF CLOTH HE HAS...

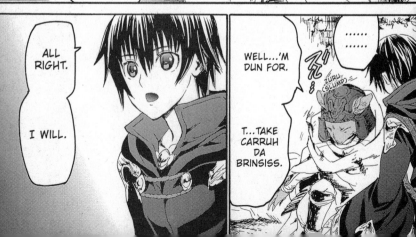

ALL RIGHT.

I WILL.

WELL...'M DUN FOR.

.....
.....

ZURU (SLUMP)

T...TAKE CARRUH DA BRINSISS.

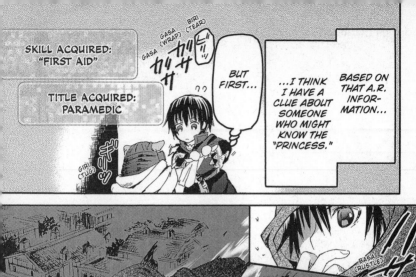

SKILL ACQUIRED:
"FIRST AID"

TITLE ACQUIRED:
PARAMEDIC

GASA
(WRAP)

BIRI
(TEAR)

GASA
(WRAP)

GIRI
(TUG)

BUT FIRST...

...I THINK I HAVE A CLUE ABOUT SOMEONE WHO MIGHT KNOW THE "PRINCESS."

BASED ON THAT A.R. INFORMATION...

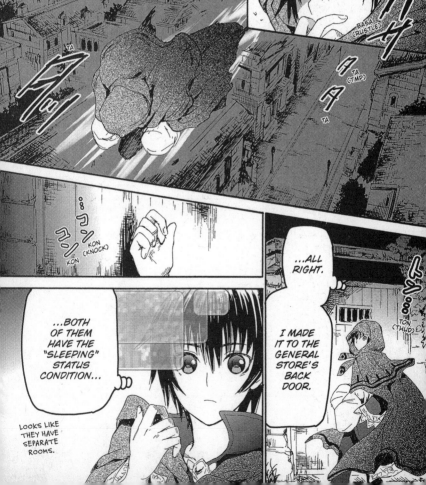

BASA
(RUSTLE)

TA
(TMP)

TA

KON
KON
KON
(KNOCK)

...ALL RIGHT.

I MADE IT TO THE GENERAL STORE'S BACK DOOR.

TON
(THUD)

...BOTH OF THEM HAVE THE "SLEEPING" STATUS CONDITION...

LOOKS LIKE THEY HAVE SEPARATE ROOMS.

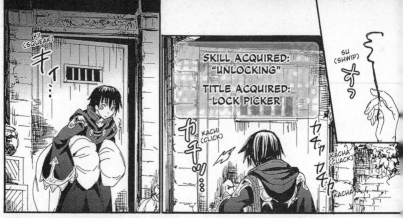

KI (SQUEAK)

キィ...

SKILL ACQUIRED:
"UNLOCKING"

TITLE ACQUIRED:
LOCK PICKER

SU (SHWIP)

ガチ
KACHI (CLICK)

カチャ
KACHA (CLACK)

KACHA

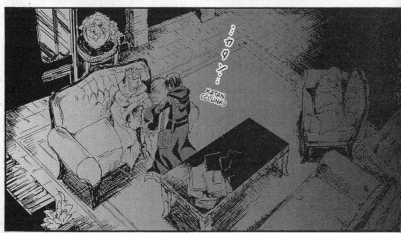

カタン
KATAN (CLINK)

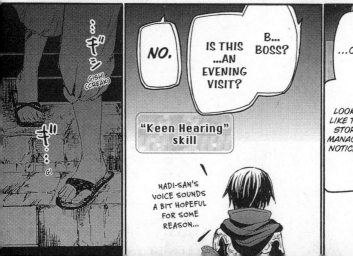

GISHI (CREAK)

ギシ...

B...
BOSS?

IS THIS
...AN
EVENING
VISIT?

NO.

"Keen Hearing" skill

NADI-SAN'S
VOICE SOUNDS
A BIT HOPEFUL
FOR SOME
REASON...

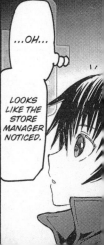

...OH...

LOOKS
LIKE THE
STORE
MANAGER
NOTICED.

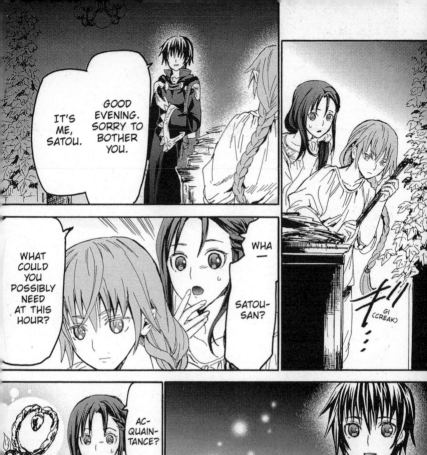

IT'S ME, SATOU. GOOD EVENING. SORRY TO BOTHER YOU.

WHA—

SATOU-SAN?

WHAT COULD YOU POSSIBLY NEED AT THIS HOUR?

GI (CREAK)

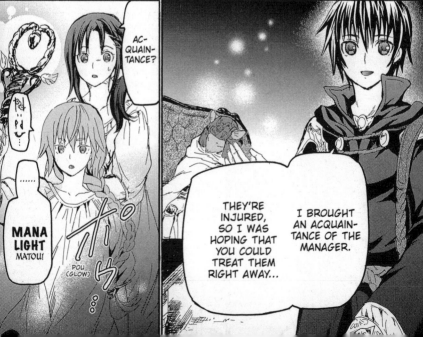

AC-QUAIN-TANCE?

MANA LIGHT MATOU!

......

POU (GLOW)

THEY'RE INJURED, SO I WAS HOPING THAT YOU COULD TREAT THEM RIGHT AWAY...

I BROUGHT AN ACQUAIN-TANCE OF THE MANAGER.

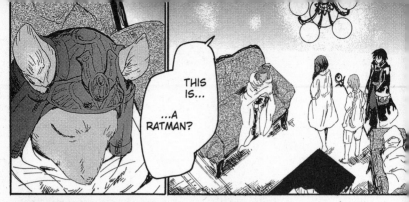

THIS IS...

...A RATMAN?

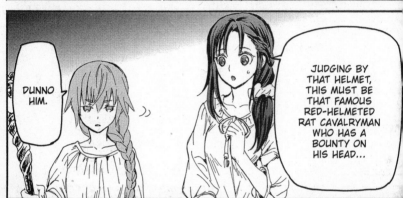

DUNNO HIM.

JUDGING BY THAT HELMET, THIS MUST BE THAT FAMOUS RED-HELMETED RAT CAVALRYMAN WHO HAS A BOUNTY ON HIS HEAD...

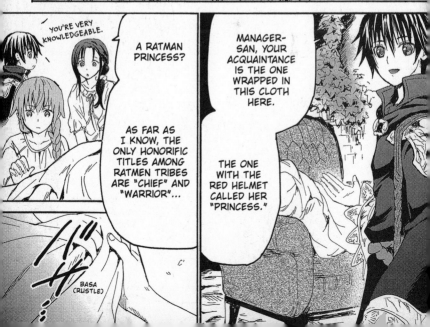

YOU'RE VERY KNOWLEDGEABLE.

A RATMAN PRINCESS?

AS FAR AS I KNOW, THE ONLY HONORIFIC TITLES AMONG RATMEN TRIBES ARE "CHIEF" AND "WARRIOR"...

MANAGER-SAN, YOUR ACQUAINTANCE IS THE ONE WRAPPED IN THIS CLOTH HERE.

THE ONE WITH THE RED HELMET CALLED HER "PRINCESS."

BASA
(RUSTLE)

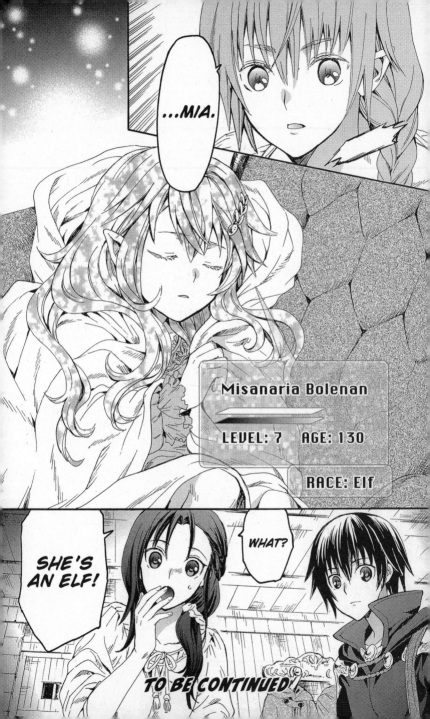

TINDER ROD

A Magic Item.
Can easily be
used by anyone.
There's a switch
on the handle.

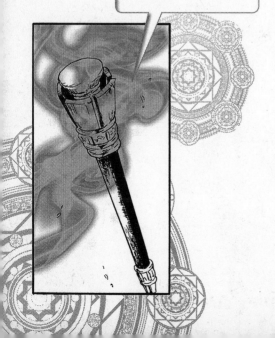

SPECIAL BONUS COMIC

NADI VISION

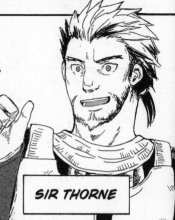

TAKING THIS ADVICE...

IT'S RIGHT ACROSS FROM THE STATION.

IF YOU RUN INTO ANY TROUBLE, GO TO THE GENERAL STORE!

SIR THORNE

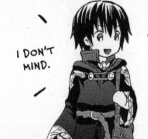

I DON'T MIND.

WOULD IT BE ALL RIGHT IF I JOINED YOU?

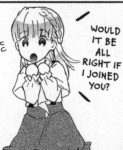

...I WENT TO THE GENERAL STORE TO ASK ABOUT A RENTAL HOUSE WHERE THE BEASTFOLK GIRLS COULD STAY.

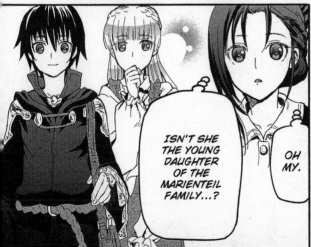

ISN'T SHE THE YOUNG DAUGHTER OF THE MARIENTEIL FAMILY...?

OH MY.

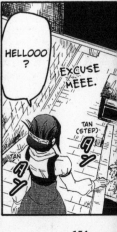

HELLOOO?

EXCUSE MEEE.

TAN (STEP)

TAN

154

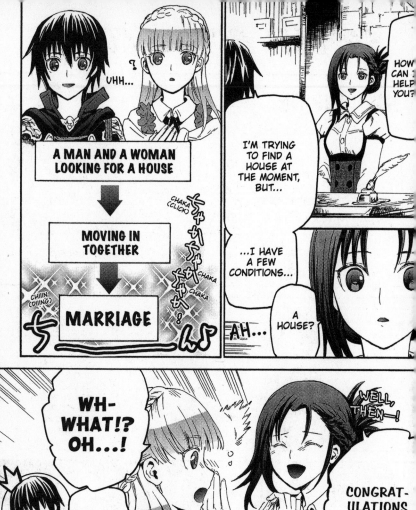

UHH...

A MAN AND A WOMAN LOOKING FOR A HOUSE

⬇

MOVING IN TOGETHER

⬇

MARRIAGE

CHAKA (CLICK)

CHAKA

CHAKA

CHIIIN (DIIING)

HOW CAN I HELP YOU?

I'M TRYING TO FIND A HOUSE AT THE MOMENT, BUT...

...I HAVE A FEW CONDITIONS...

AH...

A HOUSE?

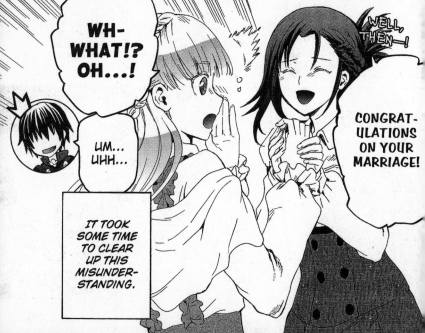

WH-WHAT!? OH...!

UM... UHH...

WELL, THEN—!

CONGRAT-ULATIONS ON YOUR MARRIAGE!

IT TOOK SOME TIME TO CLEAR UP THIS MISUNDER-STANDING.

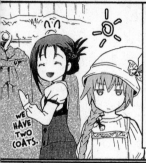

THE GENERAL STORE DOESN'T MAKE MUCH MONEY.

WE HAVE TWO COATS.

THERE ARE A LOT OF PLANTS IN THE STORE, AREN'T THERE?

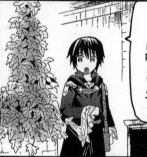

OH, THIS ONE'S GROWING NICELY!

MAYBE IT'S BECAUSE THE MANAGER IS AN ELF?

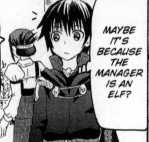

IT'S FOR FOOD!?

IT'S JUST ABOUT RIPE FOR EATING.

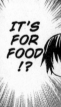

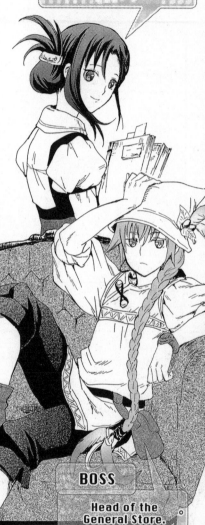

NADI

Clerk at the General Store. Very knowledgeable.

BOSS

Head of the General Store. An elf. Much older than he looks.

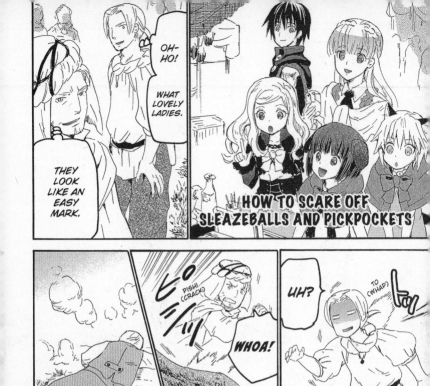

OH-HO!

WHAT LOVELY LADIES.

THEY LOOK LIKE AN EASY MARK.

HOW TO SCARE OFF SLEAZEBALLS AND PICKPOCKETS

PISH! (CRACK)

WHOA!

UH?

TO (WHAP)

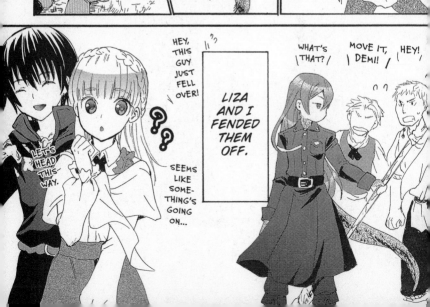

HEY, THIS GUY JUST FELL OVER!

LIZA AND I FENDED THEM OFF.

SEEMS LIKE SOMETHING'S GOING ON...

LET'S HEAD THIS WAY.

WHAT'S THAT?!

MOVE IT, DEMI!

HEY!

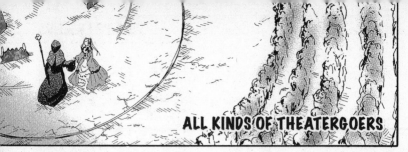

ALL KINDS OF THEATERGOERS

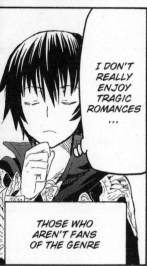

I DON'T REALLY ENJOY TRAGIC ROMANCES...

THOSE WHO AREN'T FANS OF THE GENRE

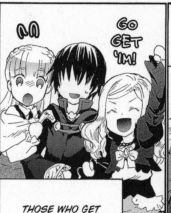

GO GET 'IM!

THOSE WHO GET OVERLY INVESTED IN THE CHARACTERS

THOSE WHO CAN'T FOLLOW THE STORY

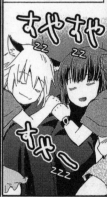

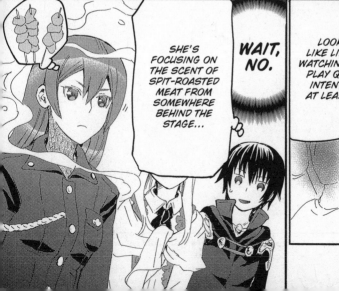

SHE'S FOCUSING ON THE SCENT OF SPIT-ROASTED MEAT FROM SOMEWHERE BEHIND THE STAGE...

WAIT, NO.

LOOKS LIKE LIZA'S WATCHING THE PLAY QUITE INTENTLY, AT LEAST...

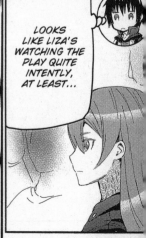

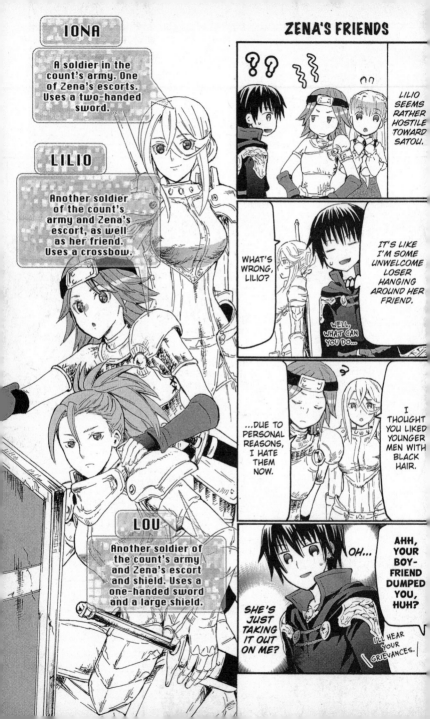

IONA

A soldier in the count's army. One of Zena's escorts. Uses a two-handed sword.

LILIO

Another soldier of the count's army and Zena's escort, as well as her friend. Uses a crossbow.

LOU

Another soldier of the count's army and Zena's escort and shield. Uses a one-handed sword and a large shield.

ZENA'S FRIENDS

LILIO SEEMS RATHER HOSTILE TOWARD SATOU.

WHAT'S WRONG, LILIO?

IT'S LIKE I'M SOME UNWELCOME LOSER HANGING AROUND HER FRIEND.

WELL, WHAT CAN YOU DO...

...DUE TO PERSONAL REASONS, I HATE THEM NOW.

I THOUGHT YOU LIKED YOUNGER MEN WITH BLACK HAIR.

OH...

AHH, YOUR BOY-FRIEND DUMPED YOU, HUH?

SHE'S JUST TAKING IT OUT ON ME?

I'LL HEAR YOUR GRIEVANCES.

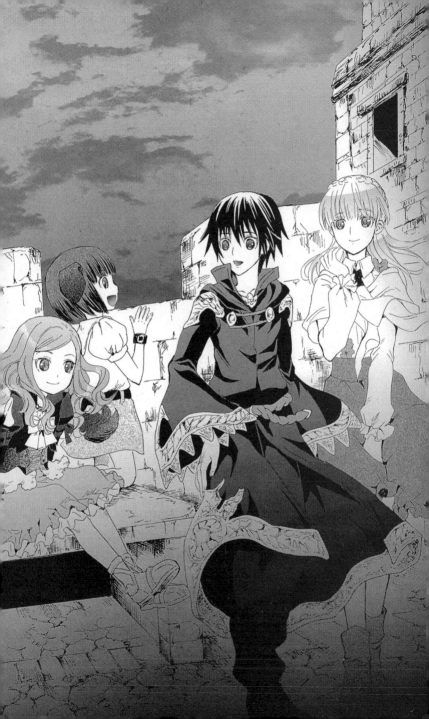

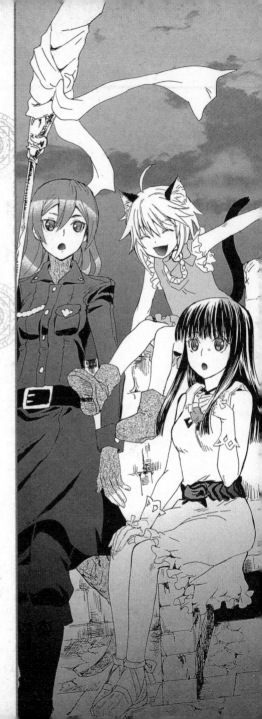

Hello again.

It's the third volume.
This one was another tightrope walk.

But I'm also kneeling in gratitude to the staff who provided me with a lifeline throughout.

I hope we can meet again in the next volume.

Thank you very much.

–Ayamegumu

...Special Thanks

● Manuscript production collaborators
Kaname Yukishiro-sama
Satoru Ezaki-sama
Yuna Kobayashi-sama
Hacchan-sama

● Editors
Toyohara-sama
Hagiwara-sama
Kuwazuru-sama

● Binding
coil-sama

● Supervision
Hiro Ainana-sama
shri-sama

● Everyone who helped with the production and publication of this book

And you!

It seemed that all the beastfolk girls liked the flower, while Arisa and Lulu didn't know about it. Maybe was local to the Shiga Kingdom.

"Ooh, in that case, why don't we all eat them together once they wilt?"

"'kaaay!"

"Yes, miss!"

Tama and Pochi hopped up and down excitedly at Arisa's suggestion.

~ A few days later ~

"They must be just about ready to eat, no?"

"Yes, I believe they are."

Liza nodded at Arisa's question.

"So, how exactly do you eat them?"

"Whooole!"

"If you eat the flower whole, you'll get the deliciousness of the crunchy petals mixed in, miss."

Tama's response was simple, while Pochi had given a more detailed explanation of how to eat the sakura plum flowers.

"Well, time to give it a try!"

Arisa bit into the flower with an earnest expression, which quickly turned into a more complicated one.

"Yummyyy!"

"Sakura plums are so tasty, aren't they, miss?"

In response, Arisa's brow furrowed deeply.

"Say, you two...which do you like better, honeyed pastries or sakura plums?"

"Honeyed pastriiies!"

"Honeyed pastries, of course, miss!"

Tama and Pochi's responses were immediate, as if it was quite obvious.

"Ah, I suspected as much..."

Arisa's shoulders sagged.

I gathered from her behavior that they weren't particularly good, but Lulu and I still tasted the sakura plums ourselves for future reference.

It was sort of like eating dried-out lettuce with a thin coating of honey.

Still...looking at the enjoyment on the beastfolk girls' faces, it wasn't too hard to eat them.

"I bet this would go great with blue-green tea if we made it into jam or preserves."

"I do not know how to make jam myself, but I can certainly inquire with the chef at the inn. Lulu, would you be willing to help?"

"Y...yes, I'll do my best!"

It sounded like Liza and Lulu would be happy to act on my simple suggestion.

As we were having this conversation, Pochi munched on sakura plum flowers while singing the praises of honeyed pastries to Arisa.

"...Are they really that delicious?"

"Aye-ayeee!"

"Of course, miss. Honeyed pastries are the taste of happiness, didn't you know, miss?"

Tama and Pochi were puffed up with pride as they responded, as if Arisa had asked a very foolish question.

"Master, I want to try these honeyed pastries as a palate cleanser!"

"Sure. Tama and Pochi, you want some too, right?"

"Aye!"

"Honeyed pastries are my specialty, sir!"

In accordance with the kids' request, it was decided that we would all go get honeyed pastries from the food cart.

Naturally, the honeyed pastries we ate together had an excellent "taste of happiness."

A short story inspired by AYAMEGUMU's special illustration on page 2 of this volume!

SPECIAL SHORT STORY
Hiro Ainana

 ### SAKURA PLUM BRANCHES

"Stop that, Tama! You mustn't take off branches with flowers on them!"

Arisa reprimanded Tama, who was up in the tree, trying to break off another branch.

"I'm sorryyy..." Tama's ears flattened at Arisa's unexpected glare.

"Arisa, wait."

"What is it, Master? You have to scold children properly, or they won't grow up right!"

For some reason, this felt like a dispute about child-raising methods between a softhearted father and a firm mother, but it wasn't actually such a complicated situation.

Tama descended sheepishly from the top of the tree.

"You've got it all wrong, Arisa."

"What do you mean?"

"Tama is pruning extra branches off the tree because Nadi asked her to do so."

At this, Arisa's face turned red, and she pressed a hand to her forehead.

"So, in other words, I just scolded Tama for no reason when she was doing absolutely nothing wrong?"

"That makes it sound pretty harsh, but, yeah, basically."

I nodded, and Arisa leaned her head against the tree trunk before looking at Tama. Feeling her gaze, Tama quivered tearfully. It looked like she was expecting to be yelled at something fierce, probably because of the harsh treatment of a previous master.

"I'm sorry, Tama." Arisa bowed apologetically, and Tama peered up at her in puzzlement.

"Y...you're not maaad?"

Her ears were still flattened back on her head.

"Of course not! I yelled at you because I misunderstood what you were doing, so I apologize."

"'kaaay."

Arisa wiped away the tears from the corners of Tama's eyes, and the cat-eared girl seemed to cheer up at last, her ears perking back up to normal.

Pochi, who'd been fast asleep in my lap, stirred with a little yawn and began to wake up. Blinking her eyes sleepily, she noticed the branches at Tama's feet and was suddenly wide awake.

"Sakura plums, sir!"

Pochi leaped up and quickly dashed over to Tama.

"These sakura plum flowers are amazingly amazing, sir!"

Her tail wagged emphatically as she picked up one of the branches.

"What's amazing about them?"

"The flowers are pretty, of course, but once they wither, you can eat them, and they're super tasty, miss!"

Pochi seemed pleased that she'd caught Arisa's interest, because her response was full of pride and triumph.

I wish someone would clear up for me, once and for all, whether these are sakura trees or plum trees.

"Oh? I wonder if you can boil them in soy sauce like chrysanthemums?"

Don't look at me while you say that. I've only been in this parallel world for less than a month.

Instead, I decided to ask the veterans.

"Tama, Liza, do you all like sakura plums too?"

"Ayeee!"

"Yes, they're certainly a seasonal delicacy."

DEATH MARCH RHAPSODY ③
TO THE PARALLEL WORLD

Original Story: Hiro Ainana
Art: AYAMEGUMU
Character Design: shri

Translation: Jenny McKeon ◆ Lettering: Rochelle Gancio

DEATH MARCHING TO THE PARALLEL WORLD RHAPSODY Vol. 3
©AYAMEGUMU 2016
©HIRO AINANA, shri 2016
First published in Japan in 2016 by KADOKAWA CORPORATION, Tokyo. English translation rights arranged with KADOKAWA CORPORATION, Tokyo through TUTTLE-MORI AGENCY, INC., Tokyo.

English translation © 2017 by Yen Press, LLC

Yen Press
1290 Avenue of the Americas
New York, NY 10104

Visit us at yenpress.com
facebook.com/yenpress
twitter.com/yenpress
yenpress.tumblr.com
instagram.com/yenpress

First Yen Press Edition: July 2017

Yen Press is an imprint of Yen Press, LLC.
The Yen Press name and logo are trademarks of Yen Press, LLC.

The publisher is not responsible for websites (or their content) that are not owned by the publisher.

Library of Congress Control Number: 2016946043

ISBNs: 978-0-316-43962-6 (paperback)
978-0-316-51183-4 (ebook)

10 9 8 7 6 5 4 3 2 1

BVG

Printed in the United States of America